AF572121

JACKIE MASON'S AMERICA

JACKIE MASON'S AMERICA

Lyle Stuart Inc. Secaucus, New Jersey

First Edition

Published by Lyle Stuart Inc.
Published simultaneously in Canada by
Musson Book Company,
A division of General Publishing Co. Limited
Don Mills, Ontario

Queries regarding rights and permissions should be
addressed to: Lyle Stuart, 120 Enterprise Avenue,
Secaucus, N.J. 07094.

Manufactured in the United States of America

Library of Congress Cataloging in Publication Data

Mason, Jackie.
Jackie Mason's America.

1. Americam wit and humor. I. Title.
PN6162.M28 1983 818'.5402 83-4659
ISBN 0-8184-0338-1

To Jyll,
my manager and friend...
who is always there for me
with unending love and devotion

Contents

Contents

Introduction

Welcome to my book.

Make yourself comfortable. Relax. You have in your hands a fantastic opportunity to read this book. Don't get nervous. I don't intend to write a bestseller. It's not my objective in life to be a sensation. Thank God, I've been a sensation long enough. I'm a sensation every place I go. Everywhere, they're saying, "Jackie Mason? Great! Fantastic!" At the very least, "Unbelievable!" I'm only telling you this in case you think this book isn't absolutely the best thing around today. In that case I'll know it's *your* problem.

You think *I* need this? I don't need this. I happen to be writing this book as a personal favor. Thank God I have enough money to last me the rest of my life. Unless I have to buy something.

Introduction

I'm not ashamed to tell you I had a problem writing this book. My problem? I have so much talent, I didn't know where to start.

Just so that you should know, this introduction is finished and the book is beginning. I hope you have more fun reading it than I had cashing my publisher's small advance royalty check.

JACKIE MASON

New York
April, 1983

JACKIE MASON'S AMERICA

My Beginnings

I come from the lower east side of New York City and from very rough circumstances. As a matter of fact, I came from a family of fourteen children. Fourteen children. It's true!

It happened because my mother was hard of hearing. I'll explain this to you. You see, every night when it was time to retire, my father would turn to my mother and say, "Would you like to go to sleep or what?"

My mother, who couldn't hear very well would say, "What?"

And that's how it happened.

It reached the point where my father was afraid to say, "What's new?" But you see my mother is a brilliant woman. In fact, she's a genius. After fourteen children she decided to stop because she found out that every fifteenth child born in America is an Indian. She figured the Indians don't have Jewish children, so why should she have an Indian child?

I really do come from the lower east side of New York. I only mention it because, from the way I talk, most people seem to think I come from Alabama.

It's true I never knew that I would be a comedian. Hard to believe? The comedy profession didn't appeal to me as a way of life. I never thought working hard would be necessary at all, because my father himself was once a big businessman.

Unfortunately, he was ruined in the crash. Some big stock broker jumped out of a window and fell on his pushcart. He was wiped out. So my father came to me with a vicious suggestion. "Get to work," he said.

How could I work? I had no time. I knew one thing about work: it takes up your whole day.

I couldn't work even if I wanted to. All my life I've had trouble with my back. I can't get it off the bed. Besides, I found that doing nothing is harder than working. The hardest thing in the world is doing nothing. You never know when you're finished.

Is Sex Dirty?

A lot of Americans worry about what they talk about in front of a child, especially if the subject is sex. They're afraid the child will learn something from them. Of course this is foolishness because we all know that a child only learns about sex from other children.

You didn't know that? Children learn the facts of life from each other, not from adults. They learn it through games they don't even understand. Did you ever notice how every kid in the neighborhood plays doctor?

Why don't they play accountant? I never saw a kid play accountant. Even the kids who want to be lawyers play doctor. Which goes to show you, there's no sense in the whole world.

Why do I say this? Because now that I'm old enough to appreciate it, I can't get a game started.

I want to give you an example. You see, what we consider clean or dirty only comes from our own unfortunately corrupted minds. To me it's a terrible problem that sex is considered a dirty subject.

We suffer from a double standard about the whole idea of sex. Our father or mother becomes our father or mother while making love. Beautiful! the arrival of a child is celebrated. Right? But how that child was created and arrived is something that is cloaked in secrecy—they're ashamed of it. They thought it was pretty clever when they did it! I'm reminded of the boy who was with his father on the street and they saw one dog mounting another.

"Daddy, what are those dogs doing?" the boy asked.

The father thought for a minute, then said, "They're making puppies."

That seemed to be the end of that until the next afternoon when the boy inadvertantly wandered into his parent's bedroom while they were doing you-know-what.

"Daddy, what are you doing?"

The father thought for a minute, then said, "We're making a baby."

The little boy replied: "Why don't you turn her over and make puppies?"

Very few American parents have the nerve to tell a child how they came into this world. I hear it's just as bad in Albania.

I myself didn't know how I came into this world until I was twenty. My parents were ashamed to tell me. They figured if they didn't tell me, I'd never find out. Now that I know, I haven't had an opportunity to do anything with the information.

They were so ashamed to tell me, that when I found out about myself, I couldn't believe it. I really couldn't! I said to myself, "*My* mother?" Somebody else's mother, I could see. But *my* mother is a quiet woman. All her life she's been cooking and cleaning. I said to myself, "When did she have the time?!" Then I took a look at my father. I said to myself, "Him, maybe. But with my *mother*? He's got a lot of nerve!"

Playboys and Other Lucky Fellows

I don't tell off-color jokes. Slightly, but not a lot because it's not nice. After all, anybody could tell off-color jokes and be a hit. The trick is to be clean and funny. This is the trick. This trick I don't know.

I got other tricks. I can't know every trick. I must start out by telling you that according to my religion it's a sin to tell a dirty joke. As a matter of fact it's the same sin as the sin of eating bread on Passover. Did you know that?

I made that up, but now I'll tell you something which is true. Did you know that according to my religion the sin of eating bread on Passover is equal to adultery. I told this to a friend of mine. He told me that he tried them both, and he can't see the comparison.

But there is an important moral lesson to be learned from this. And that is that a healthy person doesn't have to chase thousands of girls. Do you know that? Because what's the difference between one girl and another?

Girls are all the same. That's the truth. The difference is only in the imagination of the man who has to prove his masculinity by the conquest of women. Because after all, what does a man want from a woman in the first place?

How about the second place?

He wants what he couldn't get in the first place. That's why he went to the second place. Otherwise he would stay in one place.

You lost my place? A normal man only wants one thing from a woman: companionship. Of course, I'm talking about a very old man.

I'll bet you didn't even know that sex is a sickness. There is a new attitude in the country about sex. It's even reaching the city. People have discovered that sex is bad for one. For two, great!

The fact is that whether it's good or bad is not really the question. Keep in mind that the kind of people who have good times are only enjoying themselves temporarily. They are not thinking in terms of the future. Or in terms of the essential better life. They want to have a good time for the minute.

But this lifestyle is a fraud and a deception. Because a man who chases every woman in sight may enjoy himself each time, but it's only for the minute.

Did you know that? Take any playboy; you'll notice that he's exhausted by the time he's thirty-five or forty or forty-five. Not more than fifty. All right, fifty-five. The most sixty. Could you settle for sixty-five? By that time, he's tired. And it's all from running around.

That's why I don't run around. I sacrifice the momentary pleasures. It may be hard for you to believe but, in the long run, I'm better off than Frank Sinatra. I never knew this either. Fortunately, a psychologist explained it to me.

He proved it to me this way and it makes a lot of sense. He said to me, "Frank Sinatra with all those girls—how long do you think he could go on that way?"

I said to him, "I'll ask you a better question. How long do you think that I can go on *this* way?"

I never told this psychologist the truth. I'd rather go two weeks Frank Sinatra's way than one hundred years this way. So far, nobody has made me the offer.

Adultery and Marriage or How to Find Happiness Going from House to House

We live in such a degenerate society that adultery has become a way of life today. Do you know how disgusting this is? Do you know how disgusted I feel because I can't get in on it?

Everybody gets married and everybody considers marriage the only way of life. Everybody waits for his or her friends to get married and they can't get over the whole idea of marriage. It's the family ideal; essential to the whole culture we live in.

The purpose of life in this country is to get married and have children. And the tradition of marriage dominates our whole society.

So what happens today? As soon as a couple gets married they can't wait to cheat! There's no other field of endeavor in this country where you swear and promise to do one thing even while you're thinking about doing another.

If you're a businessman and you cheat on your partner, you're ashamed of yourself. You hide like a thief, because you know people will think you're no damned good!

But if you're married and you cheat on your wife, you're proud. You think of yourself as a swinger! You're not a swinger, you're a phony bastard. That's what you are. That's right. There's nothing more disgusting than a person who would commit adultery! You swore fidelity and love to your spouse. Your life is involved with your marriage partner. Who the hell are you to cheat on her? And be proud of it, yet! You no-good!

Did you know that eighty percent of the married men cheat in America. The others cheat in Europe.

This is not only true among men. It's true among women, too. Among women right now, one out of three do it. That's right. Women cheat almost as much as men.

Men can't believe it. There isn't one man here who thinks that his wife is cheating. How do so many men find so many wives to cheat with if nobody's wife cheats? But no man can imagine that his own wife is doing at home what he is doing every place else! He could come home and find his wife in bed with a strange man. He'd say, "Awwwh, she's taking dancing lessons!"

He can't imagine anybody wanting to cheat with her. Because when he comes home in the evening she looks disheveled. He says to himself, "I *have* to. Who else would bother with her?"

He doesn't know that's just how she looks in the house for him. On the outside, he wouldn't recognize her. I know a guy who's been cheating with his own wife for ten years and he still doesn't know it's her!

Men traditionally think that they're the swingers and their wives are stuck in the apartment. She doesn't go anyplace. It wouldn't enter her mind. Because if she's not having sex with him, she's not having sex with anybody.

That's what *he* thinks. He's convinced. No man believes his wife is attracted to another man. The husband could be four feet tall with a double hernia, but in his own mind, he's Paul Newman.

That's right. He can't imagine his own wife wanting anyone else. Because she tells him every day for thirty years, "I'm tired." He believes she's tired. Even if she does nothing for a living but lay in bed all day while he works.

What the hell is she tired from? She'd have to get out of bed to take a rest! Besides, "tired" has nothing to do with it. What does he want to do with her, play basketball?"

Or she'll whisper, "Not tonight! The children!"

He can't figure it out. One child is twenty-eight and the other is thirty-two.

Or she'll say, "I just did my hair."

Does she think that he wants to attack her hair-do?

But men believe everything. You believe if your wife

married you, she loves you? Fool! She married you because she needed the money! Women get married for security, not for love. Then after they got the money they convince themselves that this guy's not bad. He looks perfect.

No woman will ever admit she married a man for his money. But how come you never see a seventeen-year-old girl with a seventy-year-old man who drives a truck?

Supermarkets

Does anybody remember fresh food?

I know a ten-year-old who believes vegetables grow in cans or in frozen food packages.

You go to a supermarket today and the largest space is taken up by dog food and soap. We must be awfully dirty people to need so much soap, but that I can understand. What I can't understand is the dog food. There are aisles and aisles of dog food.

Dogs are eating better than we are.

Do you remember those commercials with Lorne Greene and Alpo? You don't see them anymore because Lorne Greene was caught eating the Alpo.

Going to the supermarket today is a ritual. You spend all morning clipping coupons so you can get a discount from foods that in a thousand years you never would have bought without a coupon. I know a guy who can't resist buying kitty litter every time he's in the store. He doesn't have a cat but he gets double coupons from Purina.

Then there are the sweepstakes. Manufacturers are competing with each other to give you houses, yachts, new homes, checks for hundreds of thousands of dollars.

Did you ever know anybody who won a sweepstake? Every time a grand prize winner is announced it's always a little old lady in a village in Wisconsin that isn't on the map. And she's always named Mary Ellen or Emma Sue. If her last name is more foreign than Smith or Jones they won't give her the prize. They tell you that in little print in the rules but to read it you would need eyeglasses so strong that you couldn't afford them unless you won the First Prize.

Not long ago I heard that the Grand Prize in a contest that promised "$1,000 an Hour for the Rest of Your Life!" was won by mistake by a Chinese laundryman in New Hampshire. Immediately the Mafia was called in. The laundryman lived long enough to collect his first check but not to cash it.

Those coupons are designed to get you to buy something you didn't want in the first place and the sweepstakes are designed to get you to buy more of it, and to keep your mind off the prices.

Have you noticed how they price things? They've got two morons with rubber stamps and ink pads. Their job is to stamp higher prices on everything. You put a few packages in your cart and then you have to run like hell to the cash register before they can catch you with their rubber stamps.

At the checkout counter they try to take your mind off the ridiculous prices with a display of *National Inquirer, Midnight,* and those other weird newspapers.

You haven't opened the first package to take the first bite of what you've bought and headlines are facing you that promise to tell you how to lose thirty pounds in twenty minutes.

Every week it's different advice on what not to eat. Avoid wheat. Eat only meat. Eat starch. Block starch. Push protein. Think thin.

Last week they advised you to throw up after every meal. That's not too hard if you buy one of those papers.

I miss the old A & P with its cracker barrels and roaches and the Irishman who always weighed your meat with his thumb on the scale. He was an honest cheat. You knew what he was doing and there was no nonsense about coupons or sweepstakes.

Overpopulation or "It's Enough Already"

Do you know that even while you read this, we are threatened by overpopulation? This very minute! It threatens to overwhelm all of us who are already here.

There's not enough food being produced to feed the babies who are coming into this world. Overpopulation, according to the Malthusian theory, is the big menace in the world today.

Did you know that? Do you know that it's happening even while you're reading this page?

In China, there are more children being born this very

minute than in India. And in India, there are more births every minute than in Turkey. Which proves only one thing; more people talk Turkey in India than in Turkey.

Sociologists have found out an amazing thing—that in most cases children are hereditary. In other words, if your parents never had children, chances are that you won't have children either.

They found out another thing that I can't get over. A team of sociologists from Columbia University went to India to find out what's causing all these children.

They couldn't figure it out. After all why should others have more children than us? Don't we got whatever they got?

So this team went to India to find out how come. Now this team got lost. So they sent another team to look for that team. Already they've lost seven thousand teams in India. And you know what they finally discovered? They found that these lost teams are causing all the children.

They also found there's one town in West Virginia where children are being born even more than in India. It was in the papers only last week. Right now. In West Virginia. They say it's because of the railroad.

I'll bet you're asking yourself the question: "How does a railroad in West Virginia make more children?"

I'm glad you asked.

You see, the trains pass every morning in this town at 6:30 A.M. and wake everybody up. At that hour, it's too early to go to work, and it's too late to go back to sleep. So what else are you going to do at 6:30 in the morning? Television doesn't start here until 7 A.M.

Well, I don't want to get any deeper into this whole subject because it's really none of my business.

Prostitution or "Thank God for Penicillin"

You know, as soon as you have a good time in this country, everybody says you belong in jail. You have to prove you're miserable before anybody has any respect for you.

Why do you think we put prostitutes in jail, but crooks we let go? Did you ever notice that? Prostitutes go to jail. Their customers go home to read *The New York Times*.

In this country you're allowed to buy cigarettes which kill people every day. Three hundred thousand people die each year in the United States from cigarette smoking. The

United States Surgeon General proved beyond a shadow of a doubt that if you definitely want cancer, smoke enough cigarettes.

So cigarettes you can get, but you're not allowed to get a hooker.

Why should prostitution be illegal? Not every man is so handsome. What if a guy don't look so hot? What's he supposed to do, attack a building? Why is it then that under capitalism you're allowed to buy anything except a girl? For what reason? Could it really hurt you?

In this country you're allowed to buy anything. If you need a shirt you have a right to buy it. If you need sex, you don't!

What's more important, sex or a shirt?

Why is sex such a dirty thing that it's the only thing you're not allowed to buy? The most natural thing in the world is sex! Does the government have the right to protect you from enjoying yourself too much with a girl you're not in love with?

You take a girl to the movies first, then you have the right to do whatever you want. But if you didn't see a picture first, she's a prostitute!

What are you eliminating? You're eliminating the middle man. Why should the cashier in the theater get the money that the girl deserves?

Remember when the story came out that tuna fish had mercury? They immediately banned tuna fish. Cigarettes they allow. Why? Why do they allow you to smoke cigarettes which definitely cause cancer but not eat tuna fish, which *might* hurt somebody?

The same thing with saccharin. Remember when they discovered that saccharin *might* hurt somebody? They weren't sure. One monkey got nauseous in Canada. They banned saccharin immediately. But when three hundred thousand citizens die every year from cigarettes, they don't do anything. You know why? I'll tell you why. Because tobacco is the fifth largest industry in America. It's more profitable for congressmen to support the tobacco industry than your life.

On Capitol Hill, Congress subsidizes tobacco to make sure you get cigarettes. In the next room down the hall, the Surgeon-General is saying "If you smoke cigarettes you'll die!"

I've never heard the Surgeon-General say "Prostitution may cause cancer."

Let's face it. Whatever you get from a hooker, one shot and it's all over. And at least you were enjoying what you were doing while you got it.

Also keep in mind that while it's going on, you're not smoking.

Richard Nixon, Ronald Reagan and Other Presidents, Fools & Thieves

It's a pleasure to know that we live in a country that has so much to offer. In what other country could a retarded person have a chance to become president of the United States?

I'm not talking about Ronald Reagan because Ronald Reagan isn't such a bad president. Anyone who keeps laughing while the country is going down the drain must know something that we never heard about.

I notice that since Ronald Reagan became president, we have no problems. You know why? Because we don't know what the problems are. You're sure you have a serious problem but then the president is making jokes and laughing, so how bad could it be?

When President Carter was president you knew you had a problem, because he kept announcing it. And he looked like he was in trouble. Everytime you saw him, his face was drained, his eyes were glazed, and he seemed to be suffering from Excedrin headache number fifty-four. Any minute you expected him to jump out of the White House window. You figured he couldn't remember that his office was on the ground floor because he had so many problems on his mind.

But Ronald Reagan, he just keeps laughing. Do you know why? He takes care not to read newspapers. Movie scripts he could read but newspapers are filled with nothing but bad news. Why should he have to know that unemployment is up, production is down, world troubles are growing and it rained in Tennessee? Who needs it? Especially when John Wayne isn't around anymore to ride to the rescue.

So President Reagan keeps laughing. Is that so bad? We need a little happiness in the world. Do you know why I suspect he's laughing? He *still* can't believe he got the job!

Take a look at what he *doesn't* read about in the newspapers. There's oppression in Afghanistan. There's a war in Lebanon. There's trouble in Poland. And he keeps laughing!

My honest opinion is, he'd rather not know what's going on. At his age he just wants to enjoy watching his wife sing with Frank Sinatra and tell people what happened to his legs in *Kings Row*.

Do you remember when a nut named John Hinckley tried to assassinate the president so that Jodie Foster would pay more attention to him?

Do you know that President Reagan was the *only person in America* who didn't know he was shot! They told him he was shot. "All right," he said with a chuckle. "I'll just lie down for a couple of hours. I'm sure it will all work out."

All he tells us is that things are getting better. He said a fifty billion dollar deficit under President Carter was a calamity. But a two hundred billion dollar deficit under him is perfect! Not only that, but he grins and says he wants a law passed to make sure there's never again a deficit. "Ha! Ha! Ha!"

It reminds me of when President Roosevelt wanted somebody to figure out how to regulate the stock market. He looked for the biggest scoundrel and he found Joe Kennedy. Who else would better know how to stop the crooks in the stock market than a crook who'd made a hundred million manipulating stock? So old man Kennedy organized the Securities and Exchange Commission. It would be like asking Al Capone to set up a commission to fight crime.

Not that I'm against him being president! Because anytime a seventy-three-year-old man can get a job I'm happy for him. Do you know at the age of seventy-three, practically the only job you can get in this country is the presidency of the United States?

Did you know that?

Ronald Reagan couldn't become a plumber, because you need qualifications for plumbing. For the presidency of the United States you don't need a thing.

They wouldn't take a chance having him fix a toilet but otherwise in the White House he can do anything he wants to do. Why do you think the toilets in this country are working perfectly but the government is full of you-know-what?

One reason the voters never find out that President Reagan doesn't know what he's doing is because he makes sure that he holds all his press conferences on the way to the car! When the reporters ask him questions, he's got no time to open his mouth because they're yelling questions and he's running to the car.

By the time they've finished the question, he's already gone! So the only thing you see is his hair! He's smiling. He's breathing. The reporters are screaming and the president is gone.

They shout, "What should we do about the recession?"

He shouts back, "Recession? Ha! Ha! Ha!"

"What about unemployment?"

"Ha! Ha! Ha!"

So the whole country knows only one thing about the presidency: "Ha! Ha! Ha!" is his answer to every question.

The one thing about him I really admire: He might know nothing about anything else, but he sure knew how to make a successful marriage with his wife, Nancy. I don't know if you've ever heard her name, but that's it. Nancy.

Did you ever see her walk? She's a nice lady but sometimes when she walks you can't tell because nothing moves! Her smile and her body are all fixed into one position like a statue! She looks like she passed away and they forgot to tell her about it.

Not that I'm making fun of the president of the United States because I never would. I never made fun out of

President Ford because he was a great president. He was brilliant! It's true he did nothing, but at least he acted like it was all none of his business.

If he could get on a plane without an accident, he was a happy man. It was only three steps to the plane, but he couldn't learn to count them. Every time he got on a plane—bing!—off the plane—bang!—he kept crashing into himself all the time. That's why he couldn't do any harm to this country. He didn't have time. He had to spend all of his waking hours trying to figure out how to walk without having an accident!

President Johnson was right about Ford. He said Ford played football without a helmet for too many years. But he knew how to keep out of trouble and Johnson didn't. In twenty-five years in congress, Ford didn't originate one bill. Not one piece of legislation! The country was working, so leave it alone.

The only bill he remembered to pay was the one he owed to President Nixon. He pardoned him of all crimes, past, present and future!

It would be in bad taste to pick on ex-President Nixon. I love Nixon! I love a crook who knows his business. With Nixon life was interesting. Every day we'd wake up and there was something else missing; we didn't know what. I used to get up every morning and wonder if the furniture was still in the White House.

Nixon was a genius. Every two days they caught him again and every two days somebody else went to jail. And he kept saying, "I don't know what they're talking about."

My sister-in-law, who is mentally retarded, knew all

about Watergate, but Nixon didn't. And everytime he denied Watergate, his nose kept getting longer and longer.

I'm not ashamed to tell you that I myself voted for Nixon. The reason I voted for him was because I wanted him to end the war in Vietnam. Humphrey wanted to continue Johnson's war in Vietnam. Nixon kept telling us during his election campaign that he had a solution to end the war.

Everybody said, "What's the solution?" and he said, "I can't tell you now. After the election I'll tell you."

Then after he got elected, they asked "What's the solution?" and he said, "Can't remember. You see, it's all perfectly clear."

Three years later the war was still going on. They said, "Why is the killing still going on?"

"Because it has to go on," he said. "Because if we don't kill Vietnamese people, the Communists will be in Washington before you could say Alexander Haig."

You believe this? Six Chinamen on bicycles are going to invade us from Vietnam? If they wanted to come here they would have sailed from Cuba. It's only a block and a half from Miami Beach!

Who could stop them? Seven old men playing cards at the Hotel Fountainbleu? You think seven old men are gonna give up a card game to fight with Chinamen?

They're 14,000 miles away from here! How come we were the only country that was worried about them invading us? In Belgium they weren't worried. In Vienna they were making pastries. Nobody else was worried except us.

Do you know that even Canada was supporting North

Vietnam? I suggested at the time that we should eliminate the middleman. Attack Canada!

It would have been an easy war to fight. You could go over there; fight a little; come back; eat lunch; and then you could start out again! During your coffie break you could drop into Detroit and buy a car. They needed the business!

If we won the war against Canada, at least we talk the same language. We'd have somebody to talk to. What are you going to say to a Chinaman, "Can I take two from column 'A' and one from column 'B'?"

I still can't figure out what we were worried about all that time. Were we actually afraid that the Chinamen would land in this country little by little? How? Have you ever tried to land a plane at Kennedy airport? It takes six hours to land a plane there.

And where would they go if they got here? Central Park? We got guerrilla fighters there now who would wipe them out in ten minutes. Even the police don't have the nerve to go into Central Park.

That's why I say that Nixon was a great mistake. The only president we had who was *really* great was President Carter! Carter was really a great president, except for the fact that he didn't have the decency to respect the office! He used words as president that I would never use as a comedian! When Ted Kennedy said that he would run against him, the first thing that Carter said was, "I'll whip his ass!"

Do you expect the president of the United States to use terminology like "I'll whip his ass"? A man with hemorrhoids yet should have the right to say this? Carter couldn't take care of his own ass, and he's after Kennedy's already?

Do you know that Carter had hemorrhoids? Spent his whole life brushing his teeth so he could smile like Alfred E. Newman. Meanwhile the problem was further down.

Carter didn't have to whip Kennedy's ass. Why should he? Kennedy was too eager to kiss Carter's.

People asked, "Why don't you pass a bill?"

President Carter announced: "Right now, I can't pass anything!"

They asked, "Should we make preparations for war?"

He said, "There's only one preparation I depend on; Preparation H. Peanuts I could understand but wars I don't know anything about!"

Did you hear about the doctor that operated on him? A Rear Admiral!

But they tell me I shouldn't make fun of presidents. That would be in bad taste!

Johnson swindled; Nixon stole; Ford blundered; and Carter lied to us. At least President Reagan is happy. He can't remember how he got the job or what he's supposed to do, so he laughs.

Come to think of it, the joke's on us.

Travel

Did you ever notice how much Americans travel? They work day and night to buy homes and furnish them and the minute they've paid off the decorator, they take out a bank loan—and poof! they're off to see the world.

There are two kinds of travelers. One type is the take-no-chance type. These people will stay only at Hilton hotels with the American flag flying. The reason is all Hilton hotels are alike, so the minute they step into their room they know where the bathroom is.

They sit at the side of the pool or in the lobby and chat with other Americans. They never leave the premises.

"Where are we?"

"We're in Hawaii."

"Oh, I thought we were in Jamaica."

"No, that was last year. Now we're in Hawaii."

If Barron Hilton was smart, he'd build one hotel in Kansas City and keep changing the scenery each week. This week Paris. Next week Mexico. Hilton clientele never leave the side of the pool except to go to the toilet. They like their vacations without surprises.

Some travelers are more adventurous.

"How are we going?"

"We're flying Air India."

"Why?"

"It's four dollars cheaper."

On Air India, the first-class passengers are served meals and the people in the coach are given rice bowls so they can beg food from the first-class passengers.

Where do coach passengers stay? The Hilton? They wouldn't put their hands that far in their pockets to come up with the kind of money Hilton charges. Cheap is their motto. Even if the toilet is three blocks away.

I know a couple who were so busy saving money that for three days after they checked in they didn't notice that their room had no bath. That didn't bother these people. They went out and bought the kind of little plastic pool you put in your backyard so your two-year-old can stay wet and cool in the summer.

This couple filled it with sink water. They kept it smack in the middle of the bedroom so they could take a bath.

I admire thrifty travelers. To save eleven cents they'll fly to Siberia and walk back to Paris.

In Paris, they seek out hidden shops and restaurants. The shops all sell antiques made in Bensonhurst, Brooklyn. The restaurants? Are there any real French restaurants left in France?

I hear they have Kentucky Fried Chicken and Pizza Pino. They even had a McDonald's on the Champs Elysées, but the McDonald's bosses took away their franchise because they said the place is too dirty. It reopened immediately as a French hamburger joint. The owner said, "McDonald's doesn't understand about French people. We *like* dirty."

Dirty I don't know about, but I heard French people eat horses. That's true. They have special butcher shops where they sell horse meat. That's why all the horses run so fast at Longchamps.

"Listen," the owner says, to his horse, "if you run last in this race, it's off to the butcher shop."

He doesn't even speak French, but the horse understands.

If you visit France you'll notice that nobody ever smiles. It's a national tradition. If you smile, you're not a true Frenchman. Tip a French bellboy five francs and he grunts. Tip him ten francs and he grunts twice and glowers at you.

Most Frenchmen are short. They're even shorter than me. How tall could you grow on a diet of nothing but crepes suzette?

It's not like London. In London people come in all sizes but none of them are Englishmen. Do you know they searched all over London to find a real Englishman and the only one they could find was Alan King? Somebody suggested they look for Sir John Gielgud, but he was in Hollywood. He makes a movie a day.

In my hotel, the manager was a Serb, the cleaning lady was Italian, the waiters were Polish, the bellboys were Greek and the cook was Chinese. A black doorman in a red uniform unloaded my luggage and said, "Welcome to Britain."

The British talk funny. They're afraid to open their mouths. If they open their mouths they may swallow a quart of London fog. So they keep their lips together when they talk.

That way you don't know what they're saying, so you keep nodding. You can't understand them, but at least they smile, so you smile and the next thing you know you've bought six cases of Chivas Regal whiskey.

I said I wanted to see the Queen, so they took me to a nightclub full of strange men dressed in women's clothing.

Other people are not so curious. They read the guidebooks and go to museums. In the States they not only never visited a museum—they wouldn't know how to spell the word. Now suddenly they're all art experts.

I went with some people from Poughkeepsie to an exhibit by Rauschenberg. He is an American, and we wanted to show our patriotism. We saw a lot of egg crates on the floor and prune pits pasted on the wall and we "oh'd and ah'd" and then we found out the exhibit hadn't even arrived yet.

Coming home is the big thing. You get on the plane and everybody carries four hundred pounds of personal baggage. The stewardess hands you a tray containing something green and something gray. Then, before you can figure out what you're eating, they turn out the lights and show a movie.

Half the people on the plane won't pay for the headset. Do you know how many lip readers the trans-Atlantic crossings have created?

At U.S. Customs, nobody ever has anything to declare. You could be bringing home enough things to furnish a large living room but when the customs man asks, "Did you buy anything?" you always say, "Oh, maybe two dollars' worth."

And then you're home. You've been away so long you forgot how to turn on a television set.

"It's good to be home."

The next day you're reading the travel ads. "What do you think of Bora Bora?"

"No, this time let's try Greece and Tahiti."

"They're near each other?"

"No, but the airline has a special deal."

Other nationalities don't travel so much. I'm not talking about the Germans. Germans travel a lot and in bunches but that's only to practice invasion.

People think the Japanese travel a lot. Don't be fooled! I used to think so too until I learned the truth. What they do is hire a lot of Chinamen and make them up to look like Japanese. Then they send them out while they stay home making Sonys.

The president of General Motors looks around and sees what he thinks are hordes of Japanese tourists.

"We can take it easy. How can a little island like Japan compete with us when their people are all running around as tourists. We got nothing to worry about."

And they're shipping us Hondas and Toyotas.

"Do you notice how nice he looks, Sam. Do you think this Japanese man could be Jewish?"

And they're shipping us Panasonics and Mitsubishis.

Someday a bunch of Americans are going to travel to

Belgrade for the baths and Belgium for the waffles and then find they can't come home again. No room. Every inch of space in America will be filled with Japanese-made television sets, automobiles, videocassette recorders, Casio computers and Benihana restaurants.

Buy American Unless You Need Something Important Like a Pencil

We have a problem in this country. We take great pride in America and everything American and we claim that America is the greatest country in the world.

American companies tell us we should only buy American cars and American products.

They take advantage of our patriotism and use it to manipulate us into buying their products. Since foreign competition is scoring so well in American consumer sales, American companies are begging us to forget the fact that American products are terrible, and telling us to buy the bad products anyway because they're made in America.

Recently I saw a secret survey that says people who make a good living don't buy anything American!

The only Americans who buy American are those who can't afford a foreign product! I found out that the only people loyal to American products are Puerto Ricans! And as soon as they climb the economic ladder, they'll be through with American products! Forget it. They'll never buy them again.

Do you understand this?

Did you ever see people looking around desperately for an American restaurant—unless they couldn't afford a decent dinner! Every American restaurant has one thing in common: bad food.

Do you know the most popular American restaurant? It's McDonald's! The second biggest? It's Burger King! If you want a decent meal you need a French restaurant or an Italian restaurant. Did you ever hear anyone say, "I'm just dying for some American cooking?" Are there any great cooking schools in Newark? I never heard a manager of a restaurant raving about the new chef just in from Idaho!

If you're wearing magnificent clothes, you're not wearing an American wardrobe. Where do you find a rich man wearing an American-made jacket? Jackets always have great European designers. Angelo. Brioni. Yves St. Laurent. I never met a well dressed man who showed me his jacket made by Mr. Irving.

Does anyone receive an American shirt for Christmas? If

so they certainly don't get too excited about it. I hear even Mr. Arrow wears Cacharel shirts.

American designers change their names so they got a chance. Sergio Valente is a friend of mine. But his real name isn't Sergio Valente. It's Saul Greenburg! But, like he said, "Who would go to a fancy clothing store and say, 'Do you have any Saul Greenbergs?'"

Are any sexy Beverly Hills fashion models going to go bike riding in a pair of Greenburg jeans? If the jeans said they were by Greenburg, they'd be big in the Bronx, Cleveland and certain parts of New Jersey—but that would be it!

Even when you move into a new apartment building, the name of the building is most likely European. You'd think you were in Paris if you just looked at the names: "The L'Amour, The Parisian, The French Quarter," Did you ever hear someone say, "I live in the Finkelstein?"

And the designs of the interior and exterior are called, "French Provincial," and "English Colonial." I never heard someone who asked, "Is your apartment French Provincial?" being told, "No, it's early Flatbush Avenue."

Even our bathroom fixtures are European. No one has a toilet made out of Pittsburgh marble. But Italian marble? That's class for your ass.

No one flies a sink in from Cleveland; only European sinks are used in this country. People don't like going to a bathroom with an American toilet. Things from Europe have more style. The only thing in that toilet that's made in America is what you put into it. And that gets flushed away. I feel like every time I go to the bathroom here I need a passport!

Watch what happens when a family can afford to send its children to private school. The kids are practically guaranteed European educations. The richer the family, the longer the kids stay away. If they can afford it, the children will spend their entire childhood in France studying mathematics.

And who are in American schools? Walk into a New York City public school classroom. What do you find? Blacks and Puerto Ricans. And you better get out of there fast before you get mugged in the corridor.

Once in a blue moon you'll see a Jewish kid there. Do you know why? He hasn't got the carfare to get out of the neighborhood.

All the families I've run into recently carry a seven-year-old child with them who talks French! Do you think French parents send their kids to Newark schools? Did you ever hear of a French kid coming to Newark to study cooking?

Next time someone tells you American products are the best in the world, take a good look at this person. He's wearing a Swiss watch, keeping warm in an Italian designer jacket and carrying a German camera. He steps into his Mercedes, wearing a French cologne.

If he's a company man, on his lapel is a little button saying, "Buy American."

The button, of course, is made in Japan.

Income Taxes: Does the Government of the United States Depend on Me for a Living?

I don't like to pay my income tax.

To tell you the truth, I resent this country even *asking* me for money. I don't use up anything in this country. I don't go anywhere.

I buy almost nothing. And when I buy it, I pay for it, so

why should I give the Government my money? For years I couldn't make a living. I was starving. You think they sent me money for that? Never. They never even sent me a postcard to ask "Maybe you need a couple dollars?"

Did they know if I needed money or not? *They didn't care!* Not one of them. Suddenly they discovered I'm making money, they became my family.

I wouldn't mind if they asked me *once*. One time I could understand and forgive. But this has been going on now for years. I told them I gave already—ask somebody else. "I can't support you all my life," I told them, "Sooner or later you'll have to learn to stand on your own two feet. I'm not going to be here forever. What are you going to do if something happens to me? You're maybe gonna close up the country?"

I wouldn't mind if this was some poor country asking me for money. They tell me that America is the richest nation in the world. So how does it look to the outside world—all the time them coming to me for a handout?

It's ridiculous. You know what the budget was for this country last year? One hundred and eighty-seven billion dollars. You know what I gave them? Twelve dollars.

Without my twelve dollars, they couldn't get along?

I told them, "First spend the one hundred and eighty-seven billion, then if you're twelve dollars short, give me a call and I'll try to help you out."

If the poor countries ask me for money I'll be glad to help them out. If Burundi wants money, I'll be the first in line to write a small check. Their whole budget last year was six dollars. If I give them twelve dollars, they could get along for two years.

But the bureaucrats in Washington who could get along

fine without my support keep hounding me for every buck. That's what really disturbs me. I could accept it when President Eisenhower or President Harry Truman asked me for money. They were poor men who never made a comfortable living. *They* needed money. I could understand that. But President Reagan? It's hard for me to believe that he can't make a living without me. I told him, "Go back to work!" He wouldn't listen.

First of all, who could afford to support him, the way he lives? Did you see the car he bought last year with my money? A thirty-five-thousand-dollar automobile! It's a special car made to order with an open top so he can stand up. If he wants to stand up, he doesn't need a car; let him take the bus!

Did *you* tell him I wanted him to buy such a fancy car?

You know what I really resented? He came to New York from Washington just to eat lunch at the Waldorf-Astoria. Let him eat in Howard Johnson's. *I* eat in Howard Johnson's. And he works for me. *I* pay my restaurant bill with my own money!

I have to feed him at the Waldorf-Astoria? And, would you believe he invited three hundred people to lunch and I didn't know one of them! Not one!

I'm buying him lunch; let him show me the guest list. How does he know I want to invite those people? The bill for that lunch was $15,000.00. My Bar Mitzvah didn't cost that much.

You know who he invited to the White House a couple a weeks ago? Assad from Syria. *I* paid for Assad's vacation in *my* White House. Would Assad invite me to *his* house?

Do you stop to think how they spend your income tax money? They take it and spend it on things you don't even need. Half a billion dollars, of which twelve dollars was mine, went last year to build roads.

I don't even have a car.

I told them, "Buy me a car—then spend my tax money for a road." And the road that they're building isn't even in my neighborhood! I can't use that road. I couldn't use that road even if I had an automobile because from my house to that road there is no road!

Another half-billion dollars of our money last year went for a school lunch program. I ate already, and even if I hadn't eaten, do I have to go to school to get a lunch? How is it going to look to Liz Smith?

On the other hand, I said to myself, "Don't be a fool. Get a little return on your investment."

So I went into one of the schools, sat down, and announced, "Okay, I'll eat lunch as long as I'm paying for it anyway."

They threw me out. They said I was too old. At what age are you too old to eat lunch?

I said to them, "Can I have breakfast at least? I'm paying for this program. Can't I get *something*?"

Did you know that last year two million dollars of our tax money went for police protection? They take *my* money to protect police! I say, let them protect themselves. They've got guns.

I got a brother who's a crook. He depends on me for a living. Why should I wipe out my brother's business just to protect them?

What bothers me as much as anything is that they spend my money to fight fires! This is the stupidest thing in the world. You and I would never try to fight a fire with money.

"Water!" I told them. "I'll send 50 gallons of water. Stop bothering me for money!"

Sometimes when I get up in the morning, I'm already tired just from realizing that this whole country depends on me for a living!

Why Jewish Men Are Schmucks

Every Jewish husband looks nervous: Each one knows that he owes his wife money, but he can't remember why! Every Jewish husband is in debt to a yenta who isn't working. She's not working and he owes *her* money!

That's why Jewish husbands cheat so much! Italian husbands don't find it so necessary to cheat. They cheat, but they don't find it necessary. Italian wives never cheat at all, they're afraid. Italian wives never leave the kitchen.

Jewish wives can't find the kitchen. Special homes are being built now for Jewish wives: homes without kitchens. The Jewish wife sees a kitchen, she gets a heart attack. Before a Jewish wife cooks one meal she'll make twelve deals. "If I cook today, I don't cook tomorrow! If I cook tomorrow I'm off Thursday. Friday, we eat in a Chinese restaurant!"

A Jew gets married and spends the rest of his life in a Chinese restaurant. Do you know what every Jewish yenta does? She makes a deal with a Chinaman, before the wedding. I envy Chinamen because they never seem to gain weight. They eat in the same restaurants as the Jews. They eat the same moo goo gai pan. They lose weight after the meal and the Jew comes home fat. It's the same food.

Did you ever see a Chinaman gain weight? They never gain weight and they eat twice as much as you. Did you ever see the way a Chinaman eats? He picks up the bowl and throws the whole thing in his face. Do you know why they don't gain weight? They keep missing their mouths. The food goes into the mouth of the Jew at the table behind him.

I don't know why Jewish men get married at all. Thirty years ago the Jewish wife was like the Italian wife of today. She cooked for you. She cleaned for you. She worked for you.

Today when a Jewish girl says "I do" that's the last thing she does. The rest of her life she spends watching machines jumping and turning and drying. There's only one thing the machines don't do—and she doesn't do this either.

I admire the way Italian men treat their wives. The wife knows she belongs in the kitchen and she never leaves the kitchen. Go into any Italian home, it could be four o'clock in the morning; sauces are flying . . . it stinks from sauces a mile from the house.

The stupidest thing in the world you can do is to marry a Jewish woman. They always say how they take care of their husbands. You believe Jewish husbands could look the way they do if someone was taking care of them?

Jewish wives want everything for themselves but they always tell their husbands, "It's for you." "You need a vacation," they'll tell you. "You look so bad. Look at you, you need a vacation. You must have a vacation." When he says, "I can't go," she says "Okay, so I'll go alone."

Did you ever see a Jewish wife packing for a vacation? A gentile wife, if she's going on a vacation, she takes a bag, puts it on her arm and she goes. A Jewish wife starts collecting suitcases like she's packing for a world tour.

Eighty-seven pieces of luggage are laid out in front of her, and she's saying, "This is for the lobby. This is for outside the lobby. This is before I go to the room. This is what I'll wear in the room. If it rains I'll wear this, and I'll bring this for the sun or in case anybody wears the same thing, close to the same thing or almost the same thing."

Meanwhile, her husband is walking around the bedroom holding one jacket: "Isn't there room for this one jacket?" he asks.

Did you ever watch them check into a hotel room? There could be four hundred hangers in the closet but there's never a hanger for this schmuck with his one jacket.

A Jewish man is the only man in the world who is afraid to act like he belongs in his own home. He paid a million for the home and he's literally afraid to walk around in it. As soon as he steps into his house, she starts yelling, "Don't step on the rug, you'll ruin it!"

Every time he makes one move, he makes four apologies. As soon as he sits down, "Watch out! Don't sit on the couch: you'll ruin the pillows! And don't go into the bathroom, you'll ruin the sink!" Not only can't he touch it, but everything he owns is not for him, it's for the guests.

He paid for it and it's always for the exclusive use of some guests his wife met somewhere, maybe at the laundromat. I say if you fall in love with a Jewish girl, let somebody else marry her, then you can come to the house as a guest and be a happy man.

Why is it that the Jewish men who have managed to overcome the worst persecutions in their determination to become successful, who fear nothing and no one, suddenly freeze when this four-foot-nine yenta storms into the house and screams "Where were you?" He says, "Uh . . . uh . . . uh . . ."

He's trembling like a helpless idiot because she's yelling "I'm going back to my mother!" Her mother is sitting in the next room watching television.

She never says, "I'm going back to my father" because he was a smart man. He threw them *both* out!

The Difference Between Jews and Gentiles

A Jew is boss in a restaurant. Did you ever see a Jew walk into a restaurant? "All right, let me see my table . . ."

No matter which table you show him, he'll say, "You call this a table? Do you know who I am? This is a table for a man like me? First of all, I don't like to sit so far from the kitchen. It's too close to the toilet, and I don't like to face a wall. Better I should face a window. And I don't like to be so close to other tables. My wife likes to face like this, I like to face like that. And I don't like a square table. I prefer a round table."

"And I don't like a fat waitress. Don't you have a skinny waitress? This chair is too hard! Don't you have a softer chair and a higher table?"

The waiter brings him a napkin. "Why such a small napkin? Don't you have a bigger napkin? And why is the coffee so weak? Don't you have stronger coffee? I don't like half-and-half: I like cream. And why does this spoon have specks? I see a speck on the spoon! Make the speck a little higher and the glass a little lower."

And that's only the first round. Before you know it, they're settled. They finally got a table they like! Then they start looking around. "I don't know what it is, but it's very drafty in here!"

When they get the food, they fight. There's forty thousand fights—no matter what you bring a Jew, they're angry at it. Did you ever notice? Bring some cake to a Jew. No matter how big the slice of cake is, his first comment is "What happened to the portions?"

Did you ever see the size of a piece of cake they serve in a gentile restaurant? A Jew never saw this before. To him it's a cookie. No matter how big the piece of cake is the Jew feels cheated. "What happened to the portions?"

Gentiles never saw cake like that. They think it's a birthday party. The Jews are complaining and the gentiles are singing "Happy Birthday to You."

Jews and gentiles have a whole different way of life. Gentiles enjoy things that a Jew can't understand. Did you ever see gentiles when they go on vacation? They take a Winnebago, and they ride. To a gentile, a vacation is looking through a car window.

"Take a look ..." The less they see the better the

vacation. They're looking for nothing! As soon as they see empty space—"Oh wow! Take a look at this!"

"What is it?"

"Nothing!"

"How beautiful!" And when they see nothing they stare hard at it. And as soon as they see completely nothing, they've reached the high point of their vacation!

"You've got to go to Arizona!"

"Why? What do you see there?"

"Space! Space like you've never seen before!"

A Jew wants to know: "Your hotel got a lobby or what?"

If there's no lobby, the Jew checks out right away.

A gentile will look at anything. Anything to them is a party. They don't care what it is. They'll look at the tomb of the Unknown Soldier. Five hundred gentile families will go with caravans and spend hundreds of millions of dollars to look at a statue, or a tomb, or a piece of shrubbery, and then they say, "Hey, that tree there is three thousand years old!"

Nine thousand gentiles go to look at a tree. "Take a look. Did you ever see such a tree?"

And the Jews are looking at the gentiles and saying to each other, "What do they see there?"

"I don't know."

"They must see something. Do you see it?"

"No I don't see it. Do you see it?"

"Is there maybe a piece of cake over there?"

Did you ever see gentiles when they go to Europe? They come back with pictures of statues and buildings. Jews come back with information about cake. "In Vienna, I found a bakery that had cake—you never saw such cake like they have in Vienna!"

Jews show you pictures of cake. "Here's a piece of Danish you never saw, take a look at this picture of a Danish . . ."

Gentiles have to see absolutely nothing to be entertained. Did you ever see the out-of-town gentiles who visit New York City? They don't know where they are. They walk around smiling and confused. Even when they're mugged, they're happy. They think it's part of the Big City tradition.

An Italian walks around wondering who he can rob. A Jew walks around watching someone being robbed and wondering how he can become a partner. And the gentile walks around saying, "Hello sir. How nice to see you sir. Have a good day!"

They don't know where they are and they don't care. The whole world is news to them. "Come over, take a look."

"What's over there?"

"A curb. Take a look."

"What an interesting curb! Did you ever see a curb like this? Take a look."

Do you know when they're really happy? When they see a line. They don't have to know what the line is for. "There's a line. Quick! Let's get on it!"

Before you know it, four thousand gentiles are standing in the line.

"What are we waiting for?"

"I don't know, but there are a lot of people here."

And the Jews are looking at the people on line. "What are they standing in line for?"

A Jew sees a line, he immediately makes a deal. He runs to the front of the line. He says, "Listen, does anybody here need a condominium?"

Something about gentiles: nothing bothers them. And I keep wondering, are they happier or are Jews happier? I have a feeling gentiles are not only happier, but they're a lot better off because nothing bothers them. If a Jew loses a dollar and a quarter, he calls up twelve partners and nine lawyers and he's suing somebody.

Did you ever see a gentile on television after his house was wiped out by an earthquake or a flood? Every two weeks he loses his house in an earthquake.

"What happened?"

(meekly) "Well . . . you know . . . my house . . . aah."

"Why do you live here?"

"I don't know. I was born here."

"How about you, sir? Why do you live here?"

"Well, now, this has been my home for forty years."

"What happened to your home?"

"I don't know. It went that way."

Nothing bothers them.

They don't even know where their families are. Ask a gentile "Where's your son?"

"My son, he left home."

"When?"

"When he was about four and a half."

"Where did he go?"

"I don't remember. Hey Clara Lou, do you remember where our son went?"

"He don't call us. We don't hear from him."

"Why not?"

"We're so busy and he was working."

"Is he working now?"

"I don't know. I think he lost his job."

"What happened?"

"He became a hippie-yippie. We don't talk to him."

A Jew knows where his son is even when he's ninety-seven. His mother knows what time he goes to the bathroom. She knows if he ate yet, or if he didn't eat at all.

She calls him up: "Hello, there's something in your voice that tells me you didn't eat. I can tell. Admit it: you didn't eat. Is that low-life, that wife of yours, going to let you starve?"

It's not right to make fun of denominations, but let's be honest, different kinds of people do have different styles of life. It's nothing to be ashamed of.

Gentiles are great in fields where Jews stink. Take athletic activities. Go to Fort Lauderdale. Right away you know you're in a gentile area. Look around. They're flying from rivers. They're fantastic athletes. Did you ever see a Jew jumping from a diving board into a pool? Unless there's a few Eisenhower dollars at the bottom of the pool, Jews don't jump from diving boards.

I've never known a Jewish athlete. The last time I heard of a Jewish athlete was maybe twenty years ago. Hank Greenberg, thirty years ago. Mark Spitz maybe. Did you see how fast he quit? He couldn't believe it himself, he said, "I'm Jewish. This is not for me."

There was one Jew, a fellow named Grossman. He played on the Pittsburgh Steelers. Remember him? It was rare to find a Jew in football. When he was playing for the Steelers, Jews all over the country couldn't believe it. When they found out that a real Jew was playing on a football team, they started phoning each other in the middle of the night. "The Jew is playing."

"Where?"

"I don't know. Turn on the TV."

"I heard he's playing today."

"What time?"

"I don't know, look it up. I heard he's on."

Every Jewish-owned television set was tuning and turning.

The gentiles were watching two teams, and all the Jews were hollering "Where's Grossman? I heard Grossman was playing?"

When he finally came out, they all got excited: "Oh my God, that's Grossman. Look how they're chasing him on the field!"

"Why are they chasing him? Those Nazi bastards!"

"They're chasing him because he has the ball."

"What! Are there so few balls in this country? Can't they buy their own balls, those Nazi bastards? Why do they need *that* ball?"

"And look how they forgot to give him a sweater, those Nazi bastards! Call up! Demand that they give him a sweater!"

They wanted all the gentiles to go home and let a Jew walk around on the field with a ball and a sweater . . .

The Lawyer Business

When I was a smaller and younger person every mother wanted her son to become a doctor. Being a doctor was a sure thing. It kept you off relief.

Being a rabbi wasn't so bad. Being a civil servant meant you could get a chance to sleep during the day. But being a doctor? There was nothing like it.

Today, doctors take second place to the legal profession.

If you don't have an oil well in your backyard or you don't own a chain of toy stores, the third best thing is to be a lawyer.

A license to be a lawyer makes stealing legal.

Have you ever consulted a lawyer? One day I consulted a lawyer to find out if I needed a lawyer. He said "No" and sent me a bill for three hundred dollars.

Three hundred dollars! Do you know how many pretzels you could buy for that? And in Philadelphia they give you mustard with them.

Two days later I was at a party and I met another lawyer. I told him how all I did was ask this first guy if I needed a lawyer and he socked it to me for three hundred bucks.

"Can he do that?" I asked.

"Yes," the second lawyer said.

The next morning *he* sent me a bill for three hundred dollars for legal advice!

Lawyers have taken over the country. We have a movie actor president but if you look at the House and the Senate, you'll find that our senators and congressmen are mostly lawyers. Who else but a lawyer could afford the high cost of an election campaign?

Are we going to elect cocaine dealers or Lotto winners?

Okay, so it's lawyers. They make the laws. They then make their living from the laws.

What a living!

Every lawyer has a meter going and he doesn't even drive a taxi. You say "Good morning" to a lawyer and immediately he turns on his meter. The only difference between him and a taxi driver is that with the lawyer, you can't see where you're going. Most of the time he's driving the cab without you. When he presents you with his bill, you really know you've been somewhere. It must have been a beautiful journey because it's so expensive.

He says "Hello" and it costs $25. "How are you?" is at least $35. Every couple of weeks he sits down to prepare your accounting.

He charges $175 an hour. Xaviera Hollander didn't charge $175 an hour!

He figures, "Monday I think I spent five hours on this case. On Tuesday I did three hours research to discover if what I decided on Monday was right. On Wednesday for four hours I read *Gone With the Wind* to see if it would offer any guidance. Two hours more on Friday because I thought about the client while I was in the elevator.

"Last night I woke up during the night. I was worrying about how high the fee was becoming. I worried for thirty minutes but since this was after hours, that should be double time. So I figure one hour at $175."

I know one lawyer who charges you if he dreams about you. Most of the time he can't remember his dreams so he figures, "It *must* have been you because I can hardly remember your case."

Somebody named Chuck Ashman wrote a book called *The Finest Judges Money Can Buy.* The trouble is that when you get done paying the lawyer, you don't have any money left with which to buy the judge.

Recently a fellow I know was giving the judge a bribe, but he had a worried look on his face.

"What's the matter?" the judge asked him.

"Well, your honor, I originally came from Italy. There we havc a custom where you give a little gift to the judge. But each side does it and the judge rules for the side that gives him the most. I'm worried, judge. I'm giving you everything I got. I don't got no more to give."

The judge thought about it. "Young man," he said finally, "What you describe may indeed happen in Italy. But I want to assure you that here in America the judges are honorable. We *never* accept gifts from more than one side!"

There is a saying that "If justice travelled from coast to coast for ten years, she'd never find shelter in a courtroom."

Myself, I'm never afraid of the law. The judge? There I'm not so sure.

My Luxury Apartment

I have to get back to New York. I pay one thousand dollars a month rent for an apartment there and I want to enjoy it! I used to live in a different apartment but I was too ashamed to let anybody know that I paid only two hundred and fifty dollars a month for that one.

After all, how does it look, a celebrity paying only two hundred and fifty dollars? A celebrity's rent *has* to be at least one thousand dollars a month. So I searched for a luxury apartment.

I found that I could rent apartments that are fantastic! If only I could use them! I feel important because now I pay one thousand dollars a month rent.

Whoever says to me, "How are you doing?" I tell them where I live.

They say, "No kidding. That's some fancy buildiing. How much rent do you pay?"

"One thousand dollars."

"One thousand dollars! No kidding!"

Now they look at me differently. One person tells another. The word gets around. "He pays one thousand dollars a month rent. Every month!"

You know what I get for one thousand dollars a month? I get music in the elevator! Sounds like nothing to you, huh? Sounds like nothing to me, too!

I told them, "I need music in the elevator?" I told them, "I'll tell you what, I'll make a deal with you! I won't listen and you deduct it from the rent!"

They turned me down.

Do I need music in the elevator? You want me to tell you the truth? I live on the second floor! How much music am I getting by the time I get from the lobby to the second floor? Maybe two bars of *Thanks for the Memory.*

There's a madame in the top floor penthouse, she hears *my* music! Why am I running a concert for her? To get my money's worth, do you know what I have to do now? I come home an hour and a half early. Then I ride up and down in the elevator and I listen to the music.

I used to take my dates to night clubs. Now I save a fortune. I take them to the elevator. You meet a higher type person. And my dates are usually thrilled. They meet a different class of people on every floor. It's exciting to them but I don't get any privacy. And the madame in the penthouse keeps trying to recruit my dates.

Another reason they charge one thousand dollars a month is because my apartment house has one of those new fantastic lobbies. They spent a half a million dollars for the lobby. The apartment? They don't even paint it. It's nothing. The truth is that I show my lobby to everyone but I'm ashamed to take guests into my apartment.

This lobby has waterfalls flowing from the ceiling! All my life I had water falling from the ceiling, but now its a fancy thing.

You notice the apartments today? They're 1-½ rooms, 2-½ rooms, 3-½ rooms? The other half is in the lobby. I told them I don't need such a fancy lobby.

The doorman, he needs it. He lives there. Let *him* pay for it. Why should I pay? A twenty-four-hour doorman yet. I need a twenty-four-hour doorman like I need the lobby!

I use the door, tops, twice a day. How long do I use the doorman? Three minutes! The rest of the day I don't need him.

He's opening the door for other people and *I'm* paying.

I told him last week, "You can take time off; I'm leaving the city for three weeks!"

He didn't have the decency to go. I'm in show business so sometimes I return to my apartment at three in the morning. I come home, he's sleeping. He has to sleep sometime because he's a 24-hour doorman.

To him it's a bedroom; to me it's a lobby. I arrive and I have to wake him up to open the door. Then he curses me for disturbing his sleep at three in the morning. He tells me, "I don't want you coming home later than midnight!"

It's embarrassing. He's an eighty-year-old man. How does it look? He has to open the door for me. I'm ashamed.

So I open the door for *him*. Don't think he doesn't appreciate it. Every Christmas I get a beautiful present.

The amazing thing is that they don't rent these apartments to just anybody. You have to have class; you have to have a reputation; you have to be very important before they take your money from you. For a room-and-a-half, one thousand dollars.

The landlord's agent asked me, "What do you do for a living?"

I told him, "I'm an entertainer!"

He said, "Then I'd better warn you right now. I don't like loud parties!"

I said, "I didn't intend to invite you in the first place."

He said, "And another thing, you can't have children!"

I said, "I knew *that* before you told me."

Then he showed me the apartment. He said, "Take a look. Have you ever seen such a high ceiling?"

I said, "It don't look so high to me."

He said, "That's because the floor is also high!"

I said, "Well, why don't you lower the floor?"

He said, "I can't! The guy downstairs also likes a high ceiling." Then he told me: "Did you know that this apartment is soundproof and fireproof?"

I said, "If it's soundproof it *better* be fireproof! Because if someone hollers 'FIRE!' and I can't hear him, I'm in a lot of trouble!"

He started to lead me around the apartment. At the window he said, "Look, did you ever see such a view?" I said, "I don't see nothing."

He said, "Wait! She's not home yet!"

They got a million gimmicks now! In my building,

electricity you have to pay for but gas is free. So when I come home I don't turn on the electricity; I turn on the gas! Going to sleep is not so bad—but oh, that getting up! I don't need an alarm clock because the music in the elevator next to my apartment wakes me every morning.

I walked into the apartment and the agent asked: "How do you like it?"

I said "Well, the living room is certainly beautiful."

He said, "No, this is the closet. The living room is over there."

The closet is twice as big as the living room!

This is a new feature: a walk-in closet. Did you ever see one? They have to have walk-in closets. There's no place to walk in the apartment. I told them, "I don't want to walk in the closet. If I want to take a walk, I'll walk in the park, I'll walk in the street, I'll walk all over. Why do I have to walk in a closet?"

You know what I do? I hang my clothes up in the living room and I sleep in the closet!

On top of everything, I have air-conditioning all year round! I need this like I need the music in the elevator! All year round air-conditioning. I told them, "I'm only hot for two months!"

Two months I'm hot; the rest of the year I have to pay for an air-conditioner! Put it in for two months!

The landlord has no place to put it, so he keeps it in my apartment and I have to pay for it! Let him keep it in his apartment. When I need it I'll call him! I told him he should pay me for storage!

Did you notice how they always build these new apartment houses in the choice locations? I'm one block from a high school! I graduated twenty years ago! The landlord wants me to start school again just because he's got a building?

The ad said: "We're only two blocks from a church!" Do I have to convert to get into the building?

They wanted one thousand dollars in advance; one thousand dollars for rent for a month; and one thousand dollars security. That's three thousand dollars. After I handed them the money, they asked me for references.

I told them, "No. You got my $3,000. You give *me* references!"

They looked at me with suspicion.

I said, "So where do you think I'm going? You can go wherever you want. You've got all my money. I can't even afford to chase you!"

What are they worried about? Maybe they're afraid I'll steal the apartment? Where would I put it? In the basement? I live there. I can't steal the building! Did you ever try to steal a building? No matter where you put it, it sticks out!

Come Fly With Me

I happen to be an astronaut on my day off. You didn't know I was an astronaut? That's because I don't make an issue out of it. I'm not like John Glenn, who looks for publicity each time he goes up or down.

Everywhere you see pictures of John Glenn flying. Not me. You never saw one picture of me flying any place. You know why? I never went. I was about to go, but I didn't need it.

First of all, I turned them down for a very good reason. They told me I had to start out at six o'clock in the morning. Six o'clock! I'm willing to risk my life for my country, but does that mean I have to give up a whole night's sleep? I don't come home till five A.M., so how am I going to get up at six?

I told them "Make it eleven-thirty and I'll help you out."

Usually I sleep till one. I'm as patriotic as the next fellow, so for my country I'll give up an hour and a half. But a whole night I can't give up. They never lost any sleep over me, either. Besides, where am I going at six in the morning? What's the hurry? Who will notice if I show up at nine?

The greatest men and women in the history of this country were all people who slept late. Did you know that? To this day wherever you go, you see signs that say: "George Washington slept here."

Why do you think he slept in so many places? Because they kept waking him up at six in the morning!

Sure, Paul Revere got up shortly after midnight to holler, "The British are coming! The British are coming!" But as soon as he woke everyone up he went back to sleep.

And how am I going to get to Cape Canaveral? I live in New York City. How will I get there? I can't take a plane. I would like to but, frankly, I'm afraid to fly. I have to take a taxi.

Even if I make all the lights do you know what this will cost me? There's a fortune of expense involved. Someone suggested I should take a bus. I can't take a bus. How would it look? An astronaut going by bus to take a rocket up.

The whole thing doesn't make sense, and the worst thing is that it isn't even a steady job. John Glenn did a great job. The next day, they got somebody else.

Afterwards if I go to the unemployment office and I'm looking for a job, they'll ask what I do for a living? I'll tell them, "I'm an astronaut."

They'll say, "How come you're not working?"

I'll say, "It's not my season."

They'll say, "How long did you work?" I'll say, "Eighteen-and-a-half hours."

Does this sound like a recommendation for a job?

You notice they always invite married men? They never ask a guy who is single to be an astronaut. They don't have the nerve. They know a single guy won't go: he's got something to live for. A married man will go anyplace. He knows things can't get any worse.

My mother was against it. When my mother found out that they wanted me as an astronaut, she asked "Why did they pick you? You got such a great sense of direction? This job is not for you." She said, "If this job was any good, would Reagan offer it to you? He'd give it to his son, the dancer . . ."

Montezuma's Revenge

What I'm about to talk about is delicate, so if you're delicate, don't read this page.

You heard of Montezuma's revenge? In Ohio they call it "the back door trots." Whether you call it "Bali Belly," "Gut Gout," or "Haitian Hoodoo," it's the same thing.

When people come home from a trip and they say, "I got sick," you know they don't mean they had flu or the measles.

I know one tour agent who promises everything and doesn't have to deliver anything. When people arrive at the hotel, the tour guide is trained to say, "Everybody take a drink of water."

That's it! For the next three days nobody in the party dares to venture two feet away from the toilet.

A man I know is so sure he's going to get sick, he always carries a medicine kit with him. He looks forward to diarrhea. That's how he keeps his weight down. If he doesn't get sick, the trip is a failure.

Diarrhea is the best way to get to know people I have ever seen. Did you ever notice how the strangers on a tour who would never even say "Good morning" to each other, suddenly are talking about their diarrhea to anyone they can find?

These are people who normally think it's too disgusting to pick their teeth in public.

Now they're asking a perfect stranger. "Did you go four times or five times?"

"I went all night."

"My wife, she went three times. How about your wife?"

People come back from vacations in foreign lands.

"Did you see much?"

"No, but I felt a lot."

"How was the food?"

"Coming in or going out?"

Somebody should package a laxative and call it "Instant Mexico." It would save the cost of the plane ride.

Paul Revere and My Jewish Roots

I have a great grandfather who happens to be an original signer of the Declaration of Independence. And it wasn't easy for him to sign it. Because he was living in Poland at the time. But he took one look; he liked it; he signed right away.

I'll tell you another thing that my family accomplished. Did you ever hear of General Custard with his last stand? Do you know that my uncle had a stand right next to Custard? But he didn't bother with Custard—he sold pizza pie. He knew that from a Custard stand you cannot make a living today.

I don't like to show off too much about my family. I just want to ask you one question. Did you ever hear of the Boston Tea Party? Who do you think was the caterer? That also was my family.

The wrong people always get credit for the inventions in this country. I'll give you a for instance. Everybody talks about Benjamin Franklin as though he invented electricity. Ben wouldn't have thought of it if it wasn't for my Uncle Abel. Uncle Abel gave him the whole idea. Franklin came to my uncle pleading for money. Uncle Abel took one look at him and said, "Mr. Franklin, go fly a kite!"

Actually, like many in my family, I'm ahead of my time. I had the same trouble Marconi had. Now you'll ask me, why do I compare myself to Marconi? Great minds have things in common. Huh? During their whole lifetime, nobody knows what they're talking about.

Years after he died they first discovered that Marconi was a great man. During his whole lifetime when he invented the radio tube nobody believed in him. Did you know that? His own wife didn't believe in him. She said to him, "A radio tube? Who needs it?"

She said, "If you're such a genius, why can't you fix the television set?"

Remember the words of Paul Revere, the only man who had the decency to get up at 4:00 A.M. just to shout, "The British are coming!"

He jumped on a horse. Strange man, he would jump on anything. He went from house to house yelling, "The British are coming!"

Everybody got excited except my great-grandmother. She said "So what if they're coming? Let them come. I got milk and cookies. Why do we have to go there every time? It's good they should come here once in a while. Who cares if the British are coming, anyway? I got nothing in common with them. Call me again when the Yiddish are coming!"

The War Between the Sexes
Part One

When a man is looking for a girl, he admits it. He'll say, "I came here to look for a broad."

If you walk into one of those singles bars that are notorious for pick-ups, the men admit they're looking for girls, but the girls never admit they're looking for men. They all pretend that they're there for anything but men.

They're squeezed against the bar, she's got a drink in one hand and her elbow in the mouth of her friend standing next to here. Twelve men are surrounding her. She's wondering which one to talk to; and she's studying all twelve of them.

But if you say to her, "What are you doing here?" she'll tell you, "Oh, I love the soup here."

"But this is a singles bar. Girls come here to meet guys."

"Others may, but not me."

"But there are twelve guys standing here talking to you."

"Can I help it if they're talking to me? Shouldn't I answer them if they talk to me?"

Every girl you meet in a bar will try to convince you she's there for a specific reason that his nothing to do with men.

Just imagine if you met a guy in a baseball uniform and he told you, "I'm not here to play baseball. I'm here because there happens to be a field here and I'm looking for shrubbery."

Women offer excuses you never heard before. Like, "Me? Oh, I was coming back from my sister's house, and she lives in Philadelphia and it so happens the only highway that runs from Philadelphia to my house passes this bar. So I figured, as long as I'm going home anyway, I'll stop in for some soup."

Or she'll say: "The only reason I come to this place is because here people don't bother me."

Did you ever hear that one? "The only reason I come to this place is because here people don't bother me."

Did you ever see a girl in a bar who would come back to that same bar if nobody bothered her? If nobody bothered her, she'd stay home. Nobody would bother her at home either, and it's cheaper.

She has to put makeup on for three hours and leave her apartment to come to a bar just to make sure that nobody bothers her?

If a girl is in the bar for two minutes and no one bothers her, she runs out.

Meanwhile, she tries to maintain the fiction that she isn't

looking for a man. If a man happens to come along, then one happens to come along.

It's like when they make love. They didn't *want* to make love. It just happened. They always tell the same story. "All of a sudden there was this guy on top of me. I don't know where he came from.

"I'm sure the door was locked. I don't even know how he got in. Maybe I locked the door after he came in? Even so, it's a mystery to me. All of a sudden—there he is!

"He's on top of me and he's panting. I think, maybe he's having a heart condition. Could I kick him out at a time like that? I planned to scream, but how could I? By that time it was too late; I was panting too."

Why do you think it is that when women have sex they don't want to *see* the sex act. Sometimes they don't even want to see the person they're doing it with.

Isn't it ironic that if a girl wants to have sex, she picks out a certain guy because he's so handsome she couldn't get over it, and she couldn't control herself, and that's why she had to make love to this man!

And then at the climactic moment, when she's gonna enjoy herself because of the magnificent quality that this face represents—she switches off the lights!

Just when she's supposed to enjoy his fantastic looks, she can't even see him! So why does it have to be *him*! It could be anybody. *It could be me!*

If you pick out a place to go for a vacation because you love what it looks like, you love the scenic beauty, would you put a bandage over your eyes when you got there so you couldn't see the beauty that you came to see? If you're not gonna see it, you might as well go anyplace! There may be a lesson in this!

I know girls don't see who they're making love to anyway, so when I want to find a girl that I want to make love to, I don't go out by myself; I go out with Robert Redford! When the girl sees Robert Redford she gets excited, and immediately she wants to slip under the covers with him.

Robert also happens to be a dear friend of mine so he does me a personal favor; Redford takes her home. They both get undressed. As she's about to do it, she turns off the lights. That's when I slip in.

Do you know how many girls think they made love to Robert Redford who had an affair with me? There's three thousand girls in Hollywood alone.

Now, all over Hollywood and even in Beverly Hills they talk about what a great lover Robert Redford is. He's making a living from this.

It wasn't Robert Redford; it was me! But please don't tell them about it. You could spoil it for me!

Men are hypocrites and liars when it comes to sex. At least that's what women say. And it's true; they are hypocrites and liars. Do you know why? Because women are so guilt-ridden about sex that they force men to lie just to be able to make love to them!

Before a girl makes love, she always asks the same thing, "Do you love me? Because if you don't love me, forget about it!"

And she's making this entire speech with her clothes off. So she says "I want to know. Do you love me? Yes or no!"

He says, "Ahhhhh . . .".

She says, "Well, I'm not saying it has to be love exactly. But I do have to know that you like me a lot. . . . Do you like me a lot?"

He says, "Ahhhhh . . . ".

She says, "I didn't say very much, all I asked you was do you like me? Do you like me at least a little?"

He says, "Ahhhhh, well . . . ".

She says, "Close enough. I'll take a chance."

The War Between the Sexes
Part Two

The truth of the matter is that women lie all the time! Not only do they lie to men—they lie to themselves. For instance, women lie in order to get married! Nice girls tell themselves they marry only because they're in love!

If love is the only reason for marriage, how come every girl gets married when she's twenty! If love was the only reason, one would get married at seventeen, another would get married at twenty-eight, one at forty-seven, one at sixty-nine. How come they're all twenty?

I know why. It's because at the age of twenty, every girl convinces herself that it's time to get married. So she decides the guy she's with at twenty is just the right guy!

And if he's not the right guy, who's to know? She'll marry him anyway!

Did you notice when she's seventeen she only wants a guy six feet tall, two hundred pounds, an Italian with a Jewish accent? He has to play basketball, tennis, fly his own plane and dance like Fred Astaire. He must be a wonderful athlete and a fantastic swimmer. A perfect person in every respect. Not even a pimple.

If you see this same girl and she's still single at thirty, she doesn't care so much if he's handsome. So long as he shows up, good enough! She doesn't care if he's passing away—as long as he lives through the wedding.

I've been talking only about the honest girls who really believe they're in love. But what about the girls who marry just for security. It's called security but they really mean cash. I never met a girl who admitted that she married a man for money. They act like it's impossible.

But how come I never saw a seventeen-year-old girl with a sixty-year-old-man who pushes a broom? Every time I see a seventeen-year-old-girl and a sixty-year-old-man, he's got twenty million dollars in each pocket!

She takes one look at him and giggles, "Isn't he cute-looking! I love the way he walks." (He can't move!) And she tells everyone who will listen: "I like an older man. You can depend on an older man." She means you can depend on him not living very long.

Or she says, "I love the way he keeps his hair." (He keeps it in his pocket.)

Did you ever see a younger girl looking into an older man's eyes? She's always looking into his eyes. He think's it's love; she wants to see if they're closing.

When she holds his hand—he thinks it's his hand—she's counting his pulse. She always claims to be so concerned about his health. And when he's got diabetes, right away she buys him boxes of Mars Bars. She tells him she wants to build up his body, so she treats him to scuba diving and snorkel lessons.

The next time you see a seventy-two-year-old man snorkeling, you can bet there's a nineteen-year-old girl sitting in his apartment checking the small print in his insurance policy.

All the old men have one thing in common; they can't believe the young women are interested in their money! This man who has negotiated with fifty thousand businessmen, and has become America's biggest tycoon after outsmarting the smartest people in the world—all of a sudden, he becomes an idiot when a seventeen-year-old chick takes a look at him and says, "Oooh, aren't you handsome!"

Twenty minutes after they're married she owns all his condominiums, all his clothes, and all his bankbooks. He's out in the cold walking around with torn underwear and he can't figure out what happened!

She took everything he owns; things that took him sixty years to get! She owns it all. All because a man doesn't want to believe he's getting old!

His wife may be getting old, but not him! He's getting younger and younger!

The Vibrator Problem

Did you know that I happen to be one of the world's greatest lovers? Most women everywhere are dying for me to make love to them. What I just said *used* to be true. Lately I've noticed a difference.

Some girls I make love to don't look so happy. And I'm talking about before, during, and after. I found out why. I discovered that there's a lot of competition around—and I don't mean other men. Or even other women.

The problem is that women have found a new way to make themselves happy that I can't compete with! They have vibrators. And there's no way a Jew like me can compete with a vibrator!

If I was twenty years younger and six times healthier, I

still couldn't compete. How could any man compete with a vibrator? A vibrator moves three thousand times each minute. I'm lucky if I can move twice a night.

This is an unbelievable situation! They gave you something to compete with where you haven't got a chance. I've heard of mechanizing industry, but I never dreamed they would mechanize sex!

Why should a girl bother with me when she can date a vibrator? She doesn't have to dress up to appeal to her vibrator. She doesn't have to put on her expensive makeup. She doesn't have to wonder whether or not she's sexy enough to turn on her vibrator. She doesn't even have to get out of bed!

The vibrator doesn't have to get turned on. All she has to do is plug it in! And the vibrator doesn't have to know whether she lost weight or not. And she doesn't have to wait for the vibrator to get excited. Or be anxious because maybe it'll climax too quickly.

The electrical plug excites it whether it likes it or not. Not only that, but the vibrator doesn't work for only two minutes or five minutes. It doesn't need *Stay Cream* or *Prolong*. As long as she pays her electric bill, the vibrator remains a faithful and active lover!

Not only that, but she doesn't have to worry that some day the vibrator will have had enough of her, and might leave her for another vibrator. And she doesn't have to worry about the vibrator cheating on her. She puts it away in the closet and it stays in the closet, waiting patiently for the next passionate encounter.

The vibrator will keep your secrets. No vibrator will sell its story to the *National Star* about how you've been doing it too often. It won't give you a bad reputation.

You could use the vibrator ten times a day. The vibrator won't whisper to people that you have a sex problem. If you have weird fetishes or want to do it in strange positions or unusual places, the vibrator won't tell. Who would it tell? Another vibrator?

A few weeks ago I found a solution in my dreams. I went out to all the neighborhood drug stores and I bought every vibrator in stock. Thousands of them.

I waited three days and then I telephoned women I know. Were they happy to hear from me! And that was after only three days! You can imagine what it would have been like a month later! All I had to do was to keep buying up vibrators.

That's when the dream became a nightmare. Soon I had thousands of vibrators. They were in every closet. I could hardly walk into the room. And believe me, it was some expensive proposition!

I'll confess something to you. Since vibrators came onto the market, I've had only one good day. Do you remember the blackout? The night of the blackout I went from house to house all over the neighborhood. You never heard such excitement!

Did it matter that I don't look like Robert Redford or Paul Newman? Not one bit. In the blackout, they couldn't see me anyway. And they couldn't use their vibrators, so any man in the dark was a life saver. All I had to do was ring the doorbell and say "Hello there!" and a woman's voice would say, "This sounds like a man—thank God!"

These days, dating for me is very difficult. If my date doesn't like my jokes, she says, "Jackie, go home!" and she goes to the nearest drug store where she can choose a red vibrator or a blue vibrator. Lately I've been hearing "Go home" so often, I'm beginning to feel like E.T.

Don't get me wrong. I haven't given up the fight. I've been trying to compete with six vibrators I know. So far the score is Vibrators 6: Mason 0.

Flying Saucers

You read a lot about flying saucers. So why is it that every time you hear that somebody actually saw a flying saucer, the sighting is always by a mentally retarded farmer from Utah?

Did you ever once hear about one flying saucer that was seen by a Jewish accountant? I never saw an accountant or a lawyer with a striped necktie and a pair of glasses say, "I just saw a flying saucer!"

Isn't it also a strange coincidence that every time someone sees a flying saucer, that person turns out to be someone who can't read or write?

This person has seen nothing in his or her life. The only thing he has ever seen is this flying saucer. And then everybody says, "So many intelligent people have seen flying saucers. They *must* exist!"

How is it that the fellow who sees saucers is always a guy who can make many sounds except speech, and when he speaks its not English, and he's lived in this country all his life! And you hear him say: "I saawww the fliiieeng saauceeer."

You can't understand him. Ordinarily, you wouldn't believe anything he says because he looks so stupid. But if he says he saw a flying saucer, you believe him.

This guy never even saw a pair of trousers because you'll notice he's wearing his pants upside down. The only thing he saw was the cow and the horse sitting next to him. Because they were there when he was born, and the next thing he saw was a flying saucer and everyone believes him.

This guy doesn't know the difference between a flying saucer and a glass of tea with lemon in it.

Crime in the Streets

Crime is a big problem today, even for the criminal. Unemployment is high, prices have gone up and people don't have much cash to carry around. On top of that, you have so many muggers that sometimes they have to mug each other just to keep in practice.

In Miami you get hit on the head if you walk on the street. I know a fellow who hires two Cubans just to walk behind him with knives pointed at him so that other muggers think he's already taken.

It's getting so bad, Cubans are even robbing Cubans.

"Stick 'em up!"

"Okay."

"You're Jewish?"

"No, I'm Cuban."

"Come on, I can tell. You're Jewish."

"I swear, I'm Cuban. I'll speak Spanish for you."

"I don't know Spanish. I didn't learn how to speak Spanish until Castro released me from prison and shipped me here."

"Honest, I'm Cuban!"

"Well, I got to take your money anyway. You look Jewish."

You could look like an enchilada in gravy but the competition is so intense that a healthy stickup man can't afford to pass up anybody crazy enough to walk along Collins Avenue.

In New York it's worse. Take, for example, night clubs. Does anybody remember the days of night clubs? The International? The Latin Quarter? Le Martinique? Billy Rose's Diamond Horseshoe?

Today the only people with enough courage to go into the streets at night are blacks and Puerto Ricans. And they won't go to night clubs. Why should they pay fifty dollars to see me when for forty-five dollars less they can go to Forty-Second Street and watch Charles Bronson shoot their relatives?

Restaurants are lucky if even the waiters come in.

They don't sing "Night and Day" anymore. They sing "Day and Day."

It's frightening.

In the old days, being a criminal was a profession. Now everybody wants to get into the business. The police are robbing warehouses in their off hours. Anytime you want a Cacheral shirt or a pair of Jordache jeans, make friends with your local policeman.

I've been following trucks for years and I never saw

anything fall out, but I have friends who have a complete wardrobe of things they got cheap because they fell off the back of a truck.

There's white collar criminals and blue collar criminals and ring-around-the-collar criminals. And they're all plotting to steal the twenty bucks I saved up for my education.

I want to return to school so I can learn to defend myself better. You heard of Kung Foo? I'm taking a course in Kong Fung.

They give you a whistle and teach you how to fight. Then they teach you the Morse code for when you're cornered and need help.

I'd rather learn the Morris code. The Morris code says, "When approached with a man holding a knife, gun or threatening note, give him everything you got. Then sell him something and get the money back."

Maybe we should persuade the criminal population to run for Congress. Who knows how to break the law better than a Congressman? And if the criminals got elected, at least it would keep them off the streets.

Jewish Astronauts

Except for me, on my day off, a Jew would never become an astronaut. Why should a Jew become an astronaut? First of all, he couldn't become an astronaut. Do you think his wife would let him go? Before a Jewish husband could go to the moon, there would be a conversation that goes something like this:

The wife demands to know, "Why are you going up there without me?

"The government told you that you have to go up there without me? Since when did the president pass a law that when you take a trip, you can't take your wife with you? You could even put it on your expense account. Why is it that every time you have to go some place, you come up with excuses. This is the best one yet!

"The government told you that you can't take me? What is this—Russia? This is a free country! Why would the government tell you not to take me? The government doesn't even know me.

"You say there is no room for me? Listen, they built cars in 1927 with room for your wife. You're trying to tell me that in this modern age when they fly to the moon, they can't find a seat for your wife? Don't make me laugh!

"In this age of technology, they can fly you to the moon but they don't have money in the budget for one extra chair? The trip costs three billion dollars. How much is a chair? A dollar twenty cents?

"*You* they're sending to the moon? From everybody in the world to go to the moon they're gonna pick you? You think you're fooling me? You're not fooling me? You have to get up early in the morning to fool me. I know what you're doing. You're going to Miami with that *shiksa*. At least you could come up with a decent excuse. You think I believe this thing about going to the moon?

"First of all if you're going to the moon, how come you didn't pack your new suit? You mean to tell me you're going to the moon dressed like that? You'll humiliate me. The neighbors will laugh at us.

"Why are you going to the moon? There isn't enough to keep you at home? There's nobody on the moon that we know. You think you'll meet the Cohens or the Schwartzs there? They're not there."

Isn't it amazing that only gentiles go to the moon?

You ask a gentile astronaut, "What are you gonna do up there?"

"Oh, we're gonna look for rocks."

Only a gentile would come back with rocks. Can you picture a Jewish husband coming home with a rock? A Jewish husband who went to the moon for two weeks would have to come home with something more than a couple of rocks. He'd have to bring at least a bracelet. Maybe a watch. *Something!* The last time a Jew came home to his wife with a rock as a souvenir he went around in bandages for a year and a half.

I'll tell you the truth: it's unfortunate for all of us that the gentiles have been the only ones in space. It's unfortunate, because they made fifty trips into space, twelve trips to the moon, and the moon is still virtually uninhabited. There's nothing there. It's because only gentiles went there. If Jews had gone, by now the moon would have twenty shopping centers and two thousand condominiums. There would be banks and beauty parlors. And lots of supermarkets with foreign foods.

And we don't have to worry about the Russians coming. There wouldn't be any space for them to park!

Five Dollars and Ethnics

I can always tell what a person's nationality is.

Most people say, "You can tell by their faces."

A lie!

There is only one sure way to tell a person's nationality and that is by watching how they shop. An Italian buys something that costs five dollars. He doesn't argue. He's scarcely aware that he pays five dollars for it. Then he sells the owner of the shop protection for five hundred dollars a month.

Watch a Polish person examine a five dollar piece of merchandise. He doesn't buy it. Do you know why? He doesn't know what it is!

An Irishman usually doesn't buy it either because he's too drunk to see it!

Did you ever see what a Jew does with a five-dollar item? He keeps looking at it and looking at it. He'll never buy it until it goes down to $4.98! He doesn't care if he has to spend forty dollars coming in from Long Island to save the two cents, but he's not going to pay full price for it. Because if there's no Sale, there's no sale!

Did you ever see what a black man does with a five-dollar item? He finds out the price. Then he goes home and waits for a race riot.

Do you know what a Puerto Rican does with a five-dollar item? He pays $3,470 for it. But he doesn't care because he only has to pay $4 a week.

I know a Jew who sold a Puerto Rican a radio thirty-seven years ago and the Puerto Rican is still paying for that radio. Meanwhile the Jew paid for three operations with the profits on that radio. He sent two children to college on that radio. He paid for his son's Bar Mitzvah from that radio. His wife had a nose job from that radio. His daughter-in-law had a hand and nail job done from that radio. Seventeen families are living off that radio! And one day he will wind up with that radio again because the Puerto Rican is gonna miss a payment and he'll get it back.

Who Puts Bibles in Motel Rooms?

Why is it that they have Bibles in every motel room? It's the most hypocritical thing I ever heard of in my life. Who checks into a motel room because they're dying to read the Bible?

Did you ever hear a guy say to a girl: "Let's check into a motel room."

"Why? What for?"

"I have this strong urge. I want to read the Bible."

"Me too! I've got that feeling too! I'm dying to read the Bible!"

Why should a man want to read the Bible when he's with a woman alone in a motel room? Why would he be interested? Whatever he's praying for, he's already got!

Who Puts Bibles in Motel Rooms?

Wander into any motel room. Notice that although the Bible is untouched, the sheets are changed every day!

What does this say to you? Doesn't it tell you that people who put Bibles in motel rooms ought to be ashamed of themselves? What could be lower or more fraudulent than putting a Bible in a motel room? What's it doing there? Would you put a double bed in a church?

If anybody did read the Bible, the only time he wouldn't need it is in a motel room. Is this a time to read a Bible? It took you three months to get her here. She's here at last and taking off her clothes. You're panting. She's beginning to pant.

Finally she turns to you and says, "Okay, I'm ready!"

What are you gonna say? "Forget about it, honey, I'd rather read the Bible."

Who could concentrate on the Bible at a time like this? I don't believe anybody ever read a Bible in a motel room.

Even if you like the Bible, you'll read it at home when there are no girls around. But to invite a girl there, tell her to take her clothes off and then read a Bible?

I fear God! But the reason I fear God is that I figure once I'm dead, I'm never gonna have such a good time as I'm going to have with this girl in the motel room.

Foreign Affairs

Israel has a new defense policy. It's the only country in the world that will fight every war without an army. From now on, if they're attacked, they won't send soldiers: they'll send a regiment of two hundred Jewish mothers to destroy the enemy with guilt.

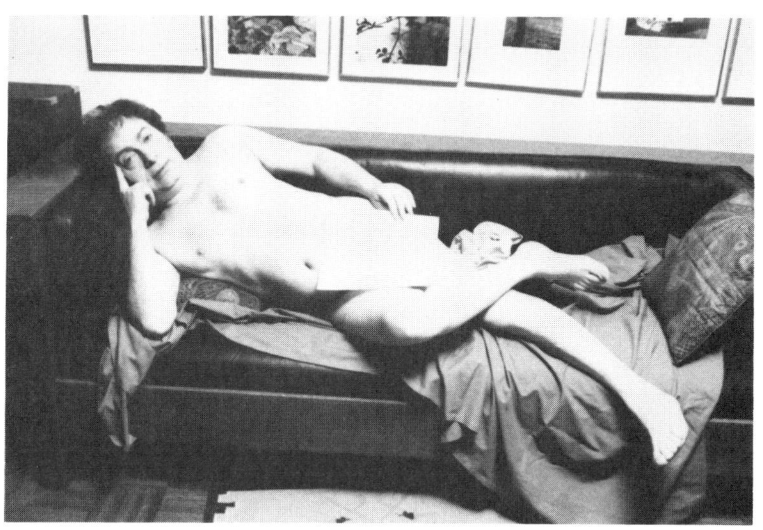

Burt Reynolds, Watch Out!

You know, before this, I never realized how much girls are in love with me. As sexy as I am, I never realized how much I was a sex object.

I've learned to recognize when a girl is in love with me.

You see, the average guy doesn't notice, but the truth is that our society is so constructed that if a woman loves a man, she's ashamed to show it. She can't. A man has to be the aggressor towards a woman at all times. As a matter of fact, the more a woman loves a man, the less likely she is to show it, because she's afraid she'll lose him.

That's how I know the girls love me. They completely

ignore me! I know one girl that's so desperately in love with me that she'll go out with *anyone* except me.

I know one girl who even married someone else just to get me jealous. She has already had six children with this guy. It still doesn't help. I *still* refuse to bother with her.

"I Could've Been a Contender"

I may not be a singer or a dancer, but I could have been a fighter.

You see, I come from a tough neighborhood. In fact, my neighborhood was so tough, the kids used to play cops and robbers with real cops, and they used to play hopscotch with real scotch! Broadjumping meant just what it says.

In my neighborhood, you had to be a fighter to survive. Walking any street, you had to have five fights before you reached the corner. It's a lucky thing I could handle myself, because the other guys I *never* could handle.

I still remember my first professional fight. I walked down the aisle and climbed into the ring. It was fantastic!

Men cheered and women screamed. I made an entrance that will never be topped by any other boxer; I had forgotten to put on my trunks.

I threw a left. I threw a right. Then another left. Another right. Then my opponent entered the ring.

Yes, it was a different kind of a fight. Right away I could see he was feeling me out. When I saw that, I decided to outsmart him. I went into a clinch. I started to feel him.

I began to enjoy it. So I said to him: "What are we fighting about? Isn't this better than fighting?"

He blew me a kiss before he punched me in the face.

I worked out a great strategy. See, a great fighter is not necessarily strong. Strategy is the most important thing. Like in the first round I started to lay low. Then he gave me a shot in the mouth. Now I was laying a little lower than I intended to. I kept my head but I lost my teeth.

I decided to dazzle him with my footwork. Meanwhile he was blinding me with his punches. My strategy wasn't working so I decided to circle him. Then he circled me. Then I circled him. Then he got mad because I was making much bigger circles than he was! (I'm not much of a fighter, but I do travel in bigger circles.)

All of a sudden he gave me another shot right in the mouth. I said to myself, "What's this? A shot in the mouth and in the middle of a circle?" And this was supposed to be my best circle!

Then I threw a right hand and punched myself right in the mouth. The sports commentator said it was the best punch of the fight.

That's when I said to myself "Jackie! You're outnumbered! It's two against one!"

Now I *really* got mad. I found an opening. Unfortunately, it was in my head. So I decided to move in on my opponent. I came back with a vengeance but he came back with a punch. So I got mad and I started to throw my famous one-five . . . one-five, one-five . . . two, three and four. I whisper all the time, "Keep in step!"

Then I came out like a caveman. He gave me one shot so I caved in.

Now one thing about me, I may go down in a fight but I'm not stubborn. If I go down, I stay there. I don't get up. I figured I'm down already so what's my hurry? Where am I going? I'm not busy. So maybe I'll rest here awhile. Because if I get up he'll only hit me again, and I'll be down here again. Why do I have to make two trips to the same place? As long as I'm lying here, I'll hang around awhile.

I noticed one other thing: as long as I was on the floor, he wasn't hitting me. I figured I should have come into the ring lying down so I never would have had this problem in the first place.

Suddenly the referee comes over and pushes him away. I looked up at him and said, "Why are you pushing now? Where were you when I needed you?"

Then he starts counting. I said "What are you counting for? I'm not getting up. Do something practical! Call a doctor!"

Who's Double Parked?

I have to tell you a true story. Yesterday, I parked my car. I walked into my house. Then I walked out. There was a cop at my car, standing with his foot on my fender—and he's writing.

I asked him, "What are you writing?"

He told me, "I'm writing you a ticket!"

I said, "Does that mean you have to put your foot on my fender? Can't you write a ticket with your foot on your own fender? You got a pen that can only write on my fender?"

He said, "I'm following orders."

So I said, "If you're following orders, then I order you to get your foot off my fender!" (I bought myself a car, I didn't buy a desk for this cop!)

I told him, "What would you have done if you were writing someone else a ticket? Where would you put your foot? Am I supposed to follow you around with my car that has a fender so you should have a place to put your foot?"

The cop said, "I'm giving you a ticket for being double parked."

I asked, "Why am I double parked?"

He said, "Because there's a car parked next to you by the curb."

I said, "Then why don't you give him a ticket? He's also double parked! As a matter of fact, if not for him, would I be double parked?! Just because he got here first, I have to pay his ticket? I don't even know the guy. Do I have to support him? Let him pay his own ticket!"

The cop said, "Don't tell it to me. Tell it to the judge!"

I said, "If I knew the judge, would I be talking to you?"

He said, "You'll have to make a personal appearance in court!"

I said, "You give me one ticket and now you think you're my manager?"

A few days later I'm standing in front of the judge, and he says to me, "Guilty, or not guilty?"

I said to myself, "If he doesn't know, why should I tell him? Let him go home and figure it out! If he figures out if I'm guilty, then let him call me back!"

He's got a lot of nerve asking me to come to court. It makes me realize that the system is just no good. I hire the police and I pay their salaries and I support their families. You know why? Because I want them to protect me from crooks! The amazing thing is that with crooks I have no trouble—I only have trouble with police!

It gets to the point where when I see a crook, I'm happy

to see him! When I see a cop, I get nervous! Were you ever out in your car and got stopped by a crook? Never! Always by a cop!

Besides, a crook doesn't pick on me. He picks on millionaires. Why should he pick on me? The crook is smart. He makes sure he's got the right guy! A crook works on a cash basis.

A cop doesn't care if he has the wrong guy. When a policeman picks on you, you'll make an appointment. A crook never makes an appointment! Besides if a crook picks on you, you can always call a cop! But if a cop picks on you, what are you gonna do? Call a crook?

Why do you think there are so many crooks running around loose today? Because the cops never go near them! They just don't bother with them! They're not in the crook business anymore: They're just out there writing tickets!

A cop doesn't need a gun. All he needs is a fountain pen. They don't study marksmanship anymore. To graduate the Police Academy you have to be good in penmanship! It's a whole new profession now.

God forbid the cops find out there's a crook in town. You think they'll look for him? Never! Why waste the time! They can make a fortune writing parking tickets! I know three cops who earn more money each day writing traffic tickets than Ernest Hemingway did when he wrote *For Whom the Bell Tolls*!

Cops can't make any money with a crook. A murderer? No profit at all. So the number of murders go up and the parking violations go down.

I sometimes think the police are afraid of murderers. Would they ask a murderer for fifty dollars? He's gonna give it to you? He's a murderer!

They don't look for murderers. They put posters all over town: "Fifteen thousand dollars reward if you catch this murderer!"

They want *me* to look for him? There's twenty-one thousand cops with guns. They're asking *me* to look for a killer! *They* want him. *I* don't want him. Let *them* look for him!

I know why they don't go out looking for murderers.

They're too tired. They exhaust themselves giving out parking tickets. I told them, "Look, I'll give out the parking tickets. You go out and look for the killer!"

They want him . . . dead or alive! Dead . . . *I'll* look. Alive . . . let *them* look. Even if I found him, what am I gonna do with him? I'm such a kaka I'm gonna walk a murderer to jail? I'm gonna tap him on the shoulder, "Excuse me, mister, I believe they want you at the police station!" He hears this, you think he's going to stroll downtown with me?

The tipoff was ex-president Nixon. As soon as he announced, "I am not a crook!" the cops started giving him traffic tickets.

How to Preach Civil Rights While Moving Out of the Neighborhood

I won't talk about black people in this book. Everybody seems to get upset when you talk about black people. You can't joke about black people. The Irish? O.K. The Jews? Why not? The Poles? Who could argue? But blacks? That's a "uh uh!"

The smartest people on earth are black people. You think you're as smart? Could *you* buy a Cadillac without having a job?

Should I tell you the truth? There's nothing wrong with

jokes about black people. Before you couldn't tell jokes about blacks because there was no real democracy. Honest. I wouldn't lie to you. *Now* we know that it makes no difference what color a person is. We don't judge a man by his religion or his color. Do you believe this so far? You do? Would you like to buy maybe the Brooklyn Bridge?

I respect black people. When I walk down a street and I see a black person coming, I cross to the other side because I respect him and I want to give him plenty of room because he might be tired and I don't want to accidentally bump into him and have him talk about my mother.

When you hear the story of *Roots* you have to have a lot of respect for blacks. All right, so maybe they copied the story. The fact is it was about a Jewish family in the garment center. That's right: it was called "Suits"!

The original story was about two Jewish women who were sitting in a beauty parlor on Flatbush Avenue. They were worried about their roots. Their regular beautician was on vacation. That's the true story. They were sitting under hair dryers and they couldn't hear each other.

One shouted to the other, "Couldn't ya hear me?"

The other shouted back, "No, I can't."

That was Kunta and Kinta.

I'm saying funny things, but to me discrimination is no joke. I'm talking to you! Who are you to persecute the black people? A man is born black—that makes him worse than you? There's *nobody* worse than you!

The blacks are a good people. I'd like to know if it's such a great thrill to be born white. How come when the sun comes out every white person is lying on the beach like a dead mackeral, desperate to turn black? Somehow, if you're born black it's no good, but if you turn black—oh ho!

The blacks fought for equality long enough. They were tired of being persecuted, so they started burning down cities. First Chicago, then Miami, then Newark, New Jersey. And that was all within 20 minutes.

That's why I say, if we had sent eight blacks to Vietnam with a pack of matches, the war would have ended in an hour and a half, instead of eight years later.

Not long ago I was in Miami. People were admiring a guy with an elegant sun tan. They couldn't get over it. "What a beautiful tan!" they exclaimed.

Then they found out he was black. Shocking! The truth of the matter is there's still plenty of discrimination in this country. We hate people we don't understand and because we don't understand them, we're afraid of them.

All over America, white people are running away from the black people. The suburbs of this country are all turning white, while the big cities turn black.

Why are the white people still discriminating against blacks! It's not just three guys named Joe. Every white is running away from even the shadow of anyone black.

I'm not talking about Lena Horne. In her case, I run the other way! But usually when a black person moves into a neighborhood, the whites join a caravan out.

And why are they running? They claim they're looking for shrubbery. People who never saw shrubbery in their lives—they see a black coming. "Whoops! Where are the trees?"

Do *you* believe they're looking for shrubbery? Those who don't claim to be looking for bushes say they're looking for better schools. Seventy-two-year-old couples claim they're looking for schools!

They don't want to mention it because it's not nice to admit it, but, the fact of the matter is, they're running away from the black people. It's not nice to say but it's true. Our culture doesn't accept us proclaiming this honestly and publicly, but that's what's really happening.

You watch a white guy in New York City who makes $180 dollars a week. A black family moves three blocks away. He panics. Right away he's in Forest Hills. Another twelve dollars, he moves to Kew Gardens. Six dollars more: Great Neck. Another four, Deer Park. He keeps going further and further out, trying to find towns that no black person would ever think of moving into.

White people are studying maps that show neighborhoods nobody ever heard of. They drive into towns where there are no homes, no shops, no trees, and no streets.

They look around.

"Take a look. Do you see a black person? You're sure? Good. This is a good city."

"You think anyone will find it?"

And you know who he means by *anyone*.

"Let's keep quiet about this place."

"From your lips to God's ear!"

"Shhhh!"

They spend all their time asking their neighbors: "Do you happen to know if anyone is buying?"

"I haven't heard."

"Are you selling?"

"No."

"Watch out!"

"I think they're coming!"

"Where?"

"I thought I saw one outside."

So everyone stands inside their houses peering through the windows.

"Do you see anyone coming?"

"No."

"I hope they're not coming."

"I heard they're buying."

"Who's selling?"

"Not me."

"Good."

As soon as a rumor starts, somebody sells.

"I heard he sold."

"To whom?"

"I heard he bought."

"He sold."

"Oy!"

If he's happy where he is, and comfortable, and he finds out nobody has bought or sold and there are no blacks coming into the neighborhood, he feels safe. He buys the house.

Now he puts a hundred thousand dollars into improving the house. Then he tells his wife to hire some help.

What kind of help?

Black, of course!

Before you know it, the couple have a black maid, a black chauffeur, a black butler—everybody running through the house is black except them. Soon they're the only white couple in the neighborhood. There's eleven black people working for them all over the place.

In the daytime go into the majority of the towns in the richer parts of this country. Notice that you don't see any white people. They're working like horses in the city to support the blacks who are living in their houses. The fact of the matter is that if they didn't work like that they couldn't afford their own houses. They got to work like horses all day and they don't even see the house in the daytime.

They just have time to come home when the sun goes down to pay the black staff.

"Here's the money," and, "Go back to work."

I visit these towns, I see all the black people. They're lying around, comfortable. They live in these mansions for nothing. What do they care? The whole house is theirs and the white guy is sweating to make enough money to pay for it.

Where does Mr. White work? In the city, of course. He works in a factory that he owns. Who works for him? Three hundred black people. He's the only white guy in the factory. And he's the only white guy in this neighborhood. But he's proud and happy. He got away from the blacks!

You see, if you live in an integrated neighborhood, you're afraid they might sneak into your house so you get nervous.

"Who knows, they might kill you!"

But if you give a black man the key and he lives there, you're safe!

Do you know the first people who came here after the Indians weren't even white? The white people think that they discovered this country. The little known fact is that the first million settlers who arrived after Columbus were black.

Did you know that?

I made it up.

Changing Horses

Did you ever hear: "Never change horses in midstream!" Do you think people know what they're talking about when they say that? Did they ever take two horses out and try to change them? I did. I'm the only guy! I once went out with two horses to the middle of a stream and I changed them.

You want me to tell you the truth? The second horse was better than the first! You know why? The second horse was lower! For years people have been saying to me, "Get off your high horse." Before this, I never really listened.

I Almost Was Drafted

Do you know I'm still suffering from shock from our last war? You want to know why? I'll tell you the truth. I was almost drafted!

I got lucky. I was wounded while I was taking the physical. When I reached the psychiatrist I said, "Give me a gun! I'll wipe out the whole German army in five minutes!"

He said, "You're crazy!"

I begged him, "Write it down! Write it down!"

Now, don't get the wrong impression. I don't want you to think that I wouldn't fight for my country. I detest a person who wouldn't fight for his own country. I would've fought for my country. I would've been proud to fight! But they called me at a ridiculous time.

I Almost Was Drafted

They called me in the middle of a war! Is this a time to call a fellow like me? I don't know what to do in peace time! Go figure out what to do with a war going on! Not that I'm a pacifist. Don't get the wrong impression! I'm not a conscientious objector, either.

I'm afraid!

Not guns. Guns don't disturb me. It's bullets I'm afraid of. I told them, "If you get a quiet war going, I'll play ball with you."

The war they were having was ridiculous! At six in the morning they started killing people. I can't see what I'm doing at that hour even without a war! Who would I shoot at? The only guy I'd like to kill is the guy who woke me up at six o'clock in the morning!

Where were the Germans going to be by nine? I found out the enemy didn't even get up till nine. Am I going to wake a guy up out of a sound sleep just to kill him? Is this nice? At least let him get up. Give him a fighting chance!

Ridiculous! To pick on me for a war doesn't make sense in the first place! I can't fight but I love my country. I want my country to have the best; not guys like me!

I told them, "There's a war going on. Is this a time to have a drop-out like me learn a trade?"

Did you know that this country has been involved in twenty-seven wars? Well, thank God, we won every single one of them without me! Now, all of a sudden, without me, they couldn't get along?

I told them, "What would you have done if I wasn't here? Would you give up?" They had eight million soldiers in the Army at the time, I told them, "First let's see how they do. If they don't do so hot, *then* I'll help you out!"

I gave them a great suggestion on how they could win

the war without me. You know that this country has prisons full of people who had nothing better to do but kill people! Thousands of murderers are sitting in prison cells right now watching television. They could be out there killing people. They're professionals!

First of all, they got their own guns! They got their own bullets! They know how to march! You don't have to give them an army serial number: they're already numbered! Just open the prison doors—let them go out and do the killing.

When I got a call from my draft board, my mother went there first. She was furious!

She said, "Why are you calling my Jackie? When he was a bum just hanging around the house you didn't want him. Now, thank God, he's working! All of a sudden you want him in the Army?" She told them, "Take my husband—he's not working!"

Then she really got mad. She told them: "Before you take my son, take me!"

So they took her! My mother turned out to be a sensation. Did you ever hear of General Alexander Haig? That's my mother! You can't tell by looking at her, she walks around like my father! She's ashamed to admit it! I'm not ashamed. I tell everybody!

The whole system is ridiculous. They promise to pay you a hundred dollars a month. Then they send you to Germany to collect it.

If the Lebanese see me, are they gonna shoot at anyone else? They weren't too crazy about me before. Now they're gonna like me? I said to myself, "Thank God they don't know where I am. I should go looking for them?"

Besides, why should I kid my own country: all my life I

see a fight I run like a thief! The bigger the fight, the faster I run! I told them, "If you need a fighter, you better get someone else. You need a runner? I can help you out!"

Some people would think that I don't love my country. All year round I work for my country in ways that most people never even think of.

That's the truth. During the Christmas season when they holler "Mail early!" I wake up at six o'clock in the morning and I mail my bills and letters. All because my country told me to mail. I don't even know what I sent or who I sent it to. I just wanted to help out my country. Every Christmas I'm the first one to mail Christmas cards. And it's not even my holiday.

Sure, I want to help my country, but they shouldn't pick on me to fight a war. I would only mess everything up.

You understand this?

Intermission

If you've been reading so far and you're not too thrilled, I'm sorry to tell you that this has no effect on my income. You already bought this book.

On the other hand, if you're not satisfied and want to send me your name and address and ten dollars, I'll send you a different book which explains what a total fool you must be if you think you're going to get your money back for *this* book!

Where Else Can a Woman Undress and Send the Bill to Her Husband?

Why does everyone tell you that their doctor is the greatest doctor in the world? How do they know he or she is the best? They all say *theirs* is the best! How do they know? All they know is that he or she managed to graduate from some medical school! That's *all* they can be sure of.

Let's assume, God forbid, that you have a kidney problem. You tell your doctor about your kidney. Do you know the grade he got in kidneys? Even if he's brilliant, how did he do in kidneys? You have no idea!

You don't need one hundred percent in every subject to

graduate! All you need is a sixty-five average. You could have a ninety-five in one subject and a thirty-five in another; it averages out to be sixty-five. Maybe, just your luck, in kidneys he got the thirty-five. He might be great for hernias. But for kidneys, you're better off with someone else.

That's why when I visit a doctor, I'm not interested in seeing his diploma; I want to see his report card! When I talk to the doctor, I ask "How did you do in kidneys?" If he says "Ninety"—great. Otherwise, on to the next office door with a doctor's shingle out.

It's not that I'm picking on doctors. Medicine is the second oldest profession in the world. First there were hookers and then came herpes, so next there were doctors.

In what other business could a man tell a woman to get completely undressed, examine her from head to foot, and then send the bill to her husband?

I know a doctor who says to every girl he treats, "Take off your clothes." I can't figure this out. He's a chiropodist.

I know a woman who went into a doctor's office. He asked her, "What's the matter?"

She says "I have a pain in my shoulder . . ."

He gave her a pelvic rubdown. She said, "Excuse me doctor, that's not my shoulder"

He said, "That's all right, I'm not the doctor!"

Medical science tells you we shouldn't smoke and we shouldn't be overweight. Did you ever notice all the fat, cigarette-smoking physicians there are in America? And that doesn't even count Brooklyn!

You go to the doctor's office and a receptionist gives you a questionnaire to fill out. Who are you insured with? Who insures them?

Where do you bank? Do you have a safe deposit box? Is it full? Are you the heir in anybody's will?

Then she asks you to sit down. You're in an office with twelve other sick people. If you sit long enough, you're sick, even if when you arrived you were well and only came to sell the doctor a subscription to *National Geographic*.

You think he has time for *National Geographic*?

The pictures, maybe. But when you are finally told to go into his office you'll find he's very busy reading *The Wall Street Journal*.

Never visit a doctor when the market is down. When the market is down, doctors are depressed and they might do anything to you to express their hostility.

They already express it when they keep you in the waiting room. That's not for your health: it's for their convenience.

That way they run a medical assembly line. The wife phones: "I need a new fur coat."

The doctor tells his nurse, "Send in four more patients."

His children call. "Dad, tuition is going up."

The doctor tells his nurse, "Send in two more."

No doctor will come to your house today unless it's to foreclose on the mortgage.

They explain: "We got the equipment *here*." They mean the billing computer.

Today if you want to get sick, you have to get sick on their schedule. Never get sick on a Wednesday or Friday. Wednesday is tennis and Friday is golf at the country club.

Not too long ago I was with some business acquaintances on the beach in Jamaica and one of them who was wading in the water happened to step on a black sea urchin. It stung him badly.

The lifeguard told us: "Somebody has to urinate on his foot. The acid dulls the pain."

We drew straws and somebody won. He pissed on the man.

We took the fellow back to his hotel. Then we called a doctor.

"What do you think we should do?" we asked.

"What do you think?" he asked.

"We don't know. That's why we're calling you."

He told us he would call us back.

He phoned five minutes later. "Have somebody urinate on it," he said. "My maid says that's the best thing you can do for it."

He went to Harvard Medical School so he could ask his maid for advice?

He was good about the bill, though. It came before we had stopped urinating.

Rubbing Girls

Did you ever hear this expression? If somebody doesn't like a person, they say: "I don't like her . . . she rubs me the wrong way."

I have a girlfriend. I'll be honest with you: she rubs me the wrong way. But I don't make an issue of it! I'm glad when she rubs me *any* way!

How to Be Happy Without Money

I don't like to make jokes about money. If I do, people get the wrong impression. As far as money is concerned, let's be honest about it. To assume that it doesn't matter is ridiculous. But to make it the most important thing in life is even more preposterous.

Money *is* important, but it's not as important as love. The most important thing in life is not money—it's love.

Personally, I'm very fortunate because I love money.

Do you know what I found out. I found out that there's only one thing you can get without money . . . sick! If you want to get better, it'll cost a fortune. Because doctors want nothing but money!

Live a life of brotherhood, honor, and fraternity, and you'll see that in the long run you'll be completely broke.

Above everything else, remember to love your fellow man. I tried to do that last night but the guy called me dirty names.

Remember too that where money is concerned, you can't take it with you. Friends are more important than money. That's why when I go, I'm going to take my friends!

Mail Order Catalogs

I've been thinking a lot about the recession. I finally figured out what caused it. It was me.

I bought a book by mail. They shipped it with a thirty-day money back guarantee, no questions asked. Twenty-nine and a half days later I sent it back. (What could I do with a book on how to breed milk goats?)

Three years later, and after forty letters, six complaints to the Postal Service Inspector and two Grand Jury investigations, my $2.98 was returned to me.

Right away they're selling my name. Did you know that the only money these catalog people really make isn't from selling the things in their catalogs. It's from renting the names of their customers.

Whom do they rent to? To other mail order companies, of course. For instance, after my name was put on the market, two thousand insurance companies rented it and sent me offerings. Magazine salesmen sent me fourteen thousand chances to win thirty million dollars in their sweepstakes. It would have taken that much money to put stamps on all their entry cards, to say nothing of paying for a subscription to *House and Garden*.

My mailbox became so full, I had to rent a small dog house so the postman could have a place to leave the mail.

Soon they assigned one mailman just to bring me the circulars.

Dish towels, tablecloths, cameras, bed pans, sex gadgets, guns, shoes—they were offering me everything. Not everybody wanted to give me things, they wanted plenty from me too.

There were armfuls of appeals for charities and causes. I learned about diseases I had never heard about. They were even asking for money for a disease caused by people receiving too much mail.

I withstood it all. I refused to be seduced by their blandishment and appeals. I didn't buy their cheeses from Wisconsin or their lobsters from Maine or their pork butts from Iowa. I didn't send money to the Retirement Fund for Richard Nixon or the 700 Club, the 1400 club or the 2100 club.

Meanwhile, the more I didn't spend, the poorer I got. It seemed that suddenly nobody had the money to pay to see me perform. Everybody was being fired. All the manufacturers were closing their plants and flying to Switzerland to join their money.

Suddenly it hit me! Catalogs were expensive. Circulars were expensive. Postage was expensive.

Renting my name had become an entire industry. Thousands of people were devoting themselves to selling Jackie Mason things by mail and I wasn't buying.

How long could this go on? The country was in a deep recession and I had caused it single-handed!

I decided to help my country. I sent a letter saying to take my name off the market. I figured I'd save all that printing and mailing.

Immediately, things got worse. I received no mail. The man assigned to deliver it was fired. The man who used to rent me the dog house went bankrupt.

I became lonely. I decided that nobody cared about me anymore. I became depressed. I was filled with guilt.

I went to a psychiatrist. He told me to buy something. Yesterday I sent $2.98 for another book on how to breed milk goats. This could be the beginning of our national recovery.

Today a fellow running for dogcatcher in a small town in Wisconsin asked me for a five-dollar contribution. I've never been in Wisconsin in my whole life but it was such a nice letter, I sent him the money anyway.

I'm hooked.

Do You Understand This?

Every woman is fooling around and so is every man. You don't believe this? It's true. Everybody you know is a swinger.

Do you know who cheats the most among the men? Not the young ones. Men seventy and eighty. The older they get, the more they cheat.

You didn't know this?

The older a man gets, the more he wants to believe he's a swinger. Especially if he's Jewish. Italians have their own problems. Regular gentiles admit they're getting older. When they're sixty years old, most gentiles forget about sex. A Jew goes just the other way.

When he's fifty he's strong; at sixty he's moving; at seventy he spends most of his time at Plato's Retreat.

He wouldn't try to make love to his wife because she's an old lady. "I don't want to hurt her . . . it's not right. She's an older woman . . . she'd fall apart."

He doesn't know that she could wipe out twelve senior citizens like him in ten minutes! Meanwhile, she's making it with the ice man and the husband doesn't even suspect it, even though they have a refrigerator!

The only reason she doesn't make love to her husband is she doesn't want to kill him! It happens to be a biological fact! A woman ages much later in life than a man. A woman is at the height of her sexual drive when she's forty-five. And she doesn't slow down till she's a hundred and two.

A man is at the height of his sexual drive when he's seventeen. When he's thirty he thanks God if his girl friend lets him watch television.

Besides, for a woman to have sex she doesn't have to be that vigorous. All she has to do is one thing: show up.

For the man showing *up* is not enough. He's got to do more.

That's where the problem is: in America the emphasis is on male sexual prowess.

A man has to prove all his life how much sex he could have. Isn't it a stupid idea that masculinity has to be synonymous with sexuality? That *I* have to be a great performer sexually?

Do you understand this?

Do *I* understand this?

Observation

Whenever there's a problem, someone always says: "Sleep on it."

I went into a butcher shop last week to buy a chicken! He showed me two chickens, and I didn't know which one I liked. He said to me, "Sleep on it." So I took the chickens home and for a week I slept with these two chickens and I *still* don't know which one I like!

There's one thing I do know: I don't sleep so good.

Lucky Dogs

Did you ever hear the expression "He lives like a dog!"?

People think that the worst thing that could happen to them, is to have to live like a dog. But do you want to know the truth—I'd *love* to live like a dog! Because a dog's life is better than mine!

If you live like a dog all you have to do is smell another dog you like and before you know it—bam!—you're already having sex.

The dog doesn't ask you to take her out. Where would you take a dog, anyway? To a dog the whole world looks the same. A dog doesn't want to see a Broadway show or attend a Frank Sinatra concert. A dog doesn't want you to spend a lot of money on her because a dog doesn't understand money.

Did a dog ask you for a dollar for the ladies' room attendant? They ask you for a bone! How much is a bone today? Not only that, but if you want to make love to a dog, do you have to check into a motel? A dog doesn't need a bed with fresh sheets and a color television set. Did you ever hear of a dog complaining about dirty sheets! As long as he's near a lawn, he's comfortable.

A dog has a great life, and you'd have a great life too, if you lived like a dog. And there's no birth control problems if you're a dog: no pills, no diaphragms.

A dog doesn't worry about whether or not she's protected. And does the mother dog ask you for child support? What's she going to do if she's knocked up—send a lawyer?

Did you ever see a lawyer that works for dogs! How could a dog locate a lawyer? Does a dog know the difference between a lawyer and an accountant! Is there a Marvin Mitchelson bulldog that we never heard about? The male dog could father three hundred puppies and then go back to Sheboygan.

Dogs have a better life in every way. They have a better life sexually. They have a better life economically; a dog doesn't have to work like a horse for a lifetime to buy a big beautiful home. *You* work like a horse all your life and you buy a big beautiful home and then you put your dog in it.

A dog doesn't save money all its life to hope someday to own a man! Why do you think dogs don't have nervous breakdowns? Because they don't have to support a schmuck like you! You get nervous breakdowns because you're supporting a wife and four children and on top of that you have to support a dog. They live off you for nothing and that's why they don't get nervous breakdowns or heart attacks.

Dogs don't even support other dogs.

They don't go out to look for apartments. They live in a dog house, they're very comfortable. I've never once seen a dog wallpapering his doghouse. They couldn't care less. They don't save up money for a car. They don't need cars. You need the car.

The dog rides in your fancy car and when he gets out he pees on it!

Dogs and People

Earlier we talked about black people in white neighborhoods. Dogs are better than people, and I'll prove it to you.

A black dog comes into the neighborhood and suddenly seven hundred white dogs look to move out? Have you ever seen seven hundred white dogs move out because they heard that a black dog was moving into the neighborhood?

A dog doesn't need a big house—he doesn't need a house at all. A dog just needs a tree. To him one tree is as good as the other; he doesn't judge the neighborhood, he judges the tree.

If the tree is big enough, he does what he has to do and he goes on to the next one. Another quality dogs have over people: a human being has to work like a horse every time he wants to do something.

If a woman has to go to the bathroom, she has to take her clothes off, she has to put her clothes on; it takes her forty minutes just to go to the bathroom. A dog picks his leg up and he's in business. He doesn't have to tip the attendant. Everything he does is easy and comfortable.

If a male dog wants to make love to a female dog, do you think the female asks him what they have in common? You think the female asks the male, "How will you feel about me in the morning?"

Do you think the female will be offended if the male dog calls her a bitch?

We go to a psychiatrist about our relationships. We have a need to learn if there's enough of a commitment. We want to find out if there's enough of involvement. Do you think a female dog cares if the male is involved?

If she appeals to him, does he think to himself, "Is this enough of an involvement?"

Does he wonder, "Should I make a commitment?"

Does one dog ever walk over to another dog and say, "What sign are you?"

A dog doesn't know the difference between an astrology sign and a "No Vacancy" sign. Any sign is good enough for him. He just wants a sign that she's ready.

If somebody says to a guy that he barks like a dog, the guy's finished. Nobody will talk to him. But if a dog barks like a dog, he's a big hit. If a dog wants to make love to another dog do you think he's going to worry that somebody might say, "You're disgusting! Get out of here—you animal!"

If a dog acts like an animal, he's a hit. She's looking for an animal. Do you think a dog is looking for an animal to act like a person? Do you think dogs ever stop to wonder if they have a meaningful relationship? A dog knows what it means; he can feel it. He wants you to mean it when you do it, that's all he knows.

Do you know what humans invest just in cigarettes alone? Every time you have sex you have to have a cigarette. If you have a lot of sex, it costs you a fortune in cigarettes.

You're a man. So first you have to pay for the hotel room. Then you have to tip the bellhop. Then you have to buy cigarettes. Then you have to wonder what to say when it's over. You can't just put on your pants and leave because you have to prove the relationship is "meaningful."

When a dog makes love to another dog, he doesn't have to meet the family. The family can't say to him, "Look what you did to my dog? Now you'll pay for it!"

A female dog doesn't have a mother who follows you around complaining "You did this to my daughter; you'll have to support her for the rest of your life!"

Somebody brings you a paper, you give him a quarter and you get rid of him. The dog brings you a paper. He doesn't even buy the paper, he just brings it to you. The mailman delivered it, he just brings it from the door to you. And all of a sudden he's being supported all his life. He doesn't do anything else—he just brings you the paper. You could walk over to the door and bring the paper in yourself. But because a dog brings you the paper, you support him for the rest of his life.

You worry maybe he'll run away. You don't worry if your wife will run away.

You give him his lunch. Then he sleeps away most of the

day. You treat this dog better than you treat your wife. If you're Puerto Rican, you're making love to your wife every day. If you're British, once a month. But in either case, at least you're getting something out of it.

What are you getting out of this dog? All he does is bring you the newspaper and twice a day maybe he wags his tail. For this it costs you more money than you're spending on your wife. Do you know that for bringing that paper from the door to the chair, it costs you seventy dollars a week? That's if he's healthy. If he's sick it's seven hundred!

Not only that, but every time he's hungry you have to buy special food for him. Your wife, whatever she cooks, she cooks for you and for her. But your dog eats food made only for dogs.

Did you ever see that dog food? It looks a lot better than anything your wife cooks.

When he brings you that paper—that dog is no dummy. I know a dog, before he goes into somebody's house he takes a newspaper with him. He knows if he brings you the paper he can live there for a month for nothing.

I wouldn't mind if after he brings you the paper he lets you read it—but three-quarters of the dogs end up going on the paper before you get a chance to read it. The paper's not even for you, it's for him. Every time you see a dog, chances are he's going on the paper.

I wouldn't mind his going on the paper if I wasn't reading it at the time. And as long as we're still on the subject of dogs, after one dog makes love to another dog he doesn't have to promise her he'll show up on Thursday. He can show up on Friday or on any day. Do you think a dog knows what day it is?

A boy dog doesn't have to worry that a girl dog will turn

him down because she's having her period. She can't say, "This is my time of the month."

Do you think a dog knows what month it is? He doesn't even know what year it is. Did you ever see a dog with a calendar? The dog doesn't know if it's 1912 or 1938. Did you ever see a dog go out and buy a calendar? You buy calendars because you want a picture of Marilyn Monroe. You think a dog knows it's Marilyn Monroe? Do you think he cares? A girl's picture can't excite a dog; he doesn't know if it's Marilyn Monroe or a picture of a horse.

If its a calendar with a picture of Lassie—well, that's a horse of another color.

Edison and God

We were taught in Sunday school that God created the universe and that it was God who said, "Let there be light," and there was light.

Good enough! But God created light only for the daytime.

I say if you want to worship somebody, worship Thomas Alva Edison! He made light at night! God didn't know how to make light at night, so while he was walking around bumping into things, he telephoned Edison and asked him to invent an electric bulb.

Edison pulled off a much bigger stunt than God because God just made an announcement: "Let there be light!"

That's no trick! Poor Edison had to stumble around in the dark where there was no light in the middle of the night, and he had to invent the light in the dark. So not only did he invent light at night but he did it without being able to see what he was doing!

Why People Should Pray Before They Eat

To everyone reading this book, I want to wish you the very best in life! And from this moment on, you should make a serious commitment to stay healthy.

My advice in this department is that you try to eat less. Because as soon as you sit down to eat, you're destroying your health so quickly that you're eventually going to die. As a matter of fact, you'll pass away faster from eating than from starving!

That's because it takes at least a day and a half to starve to death, but according to the Health Department's latest figures, "Most of the things you eat can kill you in nine seconds!"

There was a time when they said that one thing was good to eat and another thing was bad. They taught us to be selective about what we put into our stomachs. Then they found out that most any food you eat today is bad for you!

You have to be the world's greatest detective these days to find out which foods are good for you. And as soon as you discover what they are and start eating them, some research scientist announces that they're bad!

It's no longer a question of staying healthy. It's a question of picking out a sickness that you like.

They once told us that a cup of coffee wouldn't do any harm. Now they know a cup of coffee not only will do you harm but you can't believe how much damage it can cause you all around.

For one thing, it's bad for the lining of your stomach. It sits and burns the lining. And on the side, it causes cancer! Not only does it cause cancer but it also keeps you up at night worrying about the cancer.

So you're not only dying from it, but you have to stay up all night to watch yourself slowly pass away.

You think plain coffee is dangerous? Most people don't drink just plain coffee: they add a little sugar. Now they find out that sugar gives you diabetes! So if you survive the coffee, the sugar will get you.

So you say to yourself, "Diabetes is very dangerous, I'll change to saccharin."

You felt safe and healthy with saccharin. Then they announced that a drunken mouse in a cage in Calgary,

Canada, died from eating twelve pounds of saccharin in one night. So it must be that saccharin can kill you too!

Now you realize that one cup of coffee can kill you three different ways!

So you say to yourself, "I'll stay away from coffee with all those problems. I'll drink milk!"

Will they leave you alone? No chance. A young fellow who wants a Nobel Prize announces that milk causes cholesterol and cholesterol is a great contributor to heart problems.

A heart problem is not too good for you. As a matter of fact, a heart condition is more likely to kill you than cancer—and faster.

So now you have another way to go, and you didn't even eat yet!

You say to yourself, "I'll stay away from milk. Why should I take chances? I'll drink Coke!" But then you find out that Coca-Cola has more caffeine in it than coffee!

So you figure, "I'll drink tea. Tea should be the safest of all."

So they announce that tea contains more caffeine than coffee or Coke! One cup of tea will kill you faster than two coffees and three and one-half Cokes!

So you say to yourself, "I won't drink any of these things, they're all much too dangerous! I'll drink only plain sink water!"

You *know* water is good for you, right? That is, except if you drink it! They found out that water in the United States is so polluted that if you drink it, it causes cancer faster than three cups of tea, four cups of coffee and five glasses of milk put together!

Do you know how many fish commit suicide each day drinking water in our rivers?

So now you say to yourself, "To hell with water. I won't drink it. I'll stay healthy. I won't drink anything!"

So you walk around panting and sweating like a pig but, knowing that you're healthier from not drinking anything, because as soon as you touch any liquid in this country you'll pass away.

Now, you're avoiding nine ways of dying from liquids but you still haven't had a bite of food yet!

The safest thing in the world to eat is vegetables! Vegetables are healthy? They *would* be healthy if we could find a way to manufacture them in an antiseptic factory. Unfortunately we still have to grow them in dirt! And by the time the vegetables get to you they have no vitamin content.

That's because they grow them in Indonesia, so by the time they reach your table, they've lost all their nutritional value.

They grow them in Kansas, Oregon and New Jersey, too, but the government pays the American farmers to plow the vegetables back into the earth. So the farmer can make more money by plowing his whole crop back into the earth. *These* vegetables would have been excellent for you but, unfortunately, they never leave the farmer's field.

The fact is that vegetables from Indonesia won't do you any good at all. With the vitamins out, the only thing left in is their taste, and that's not too good. The farmers put so much DDT's and PCB's and BVD's on them to make sure they're the right color and to make sure the insects won't get to them, so they can grow safely. But the problem with that is that not only do the insects die from eating these chemicals—we do too! So they're preserving vegetables and killing us!

The insect dies. You die. And the vegetable stays healthy.

The only way that a vegetable is good for you is if you put it in a flower pot by the window and you sit there quietly and watch it grow.

But I have good news. Not all vegetables are bad for you. Vegetables are safe for you to eat when they are grown on a certain farm that promotes natural growth. There they don't care if insects come around or not.

Maybe only one vegetable survives, but that one vegetable is excellent for you. Provided, of course, that you eat it there and then and don't try to take it home with you. If you take it out, that's different. Then it may get germs on it from air pollution.

The trouble is nobody can make a living growing vegetables that way. So to find one good vegetable, you have to find a farm where they grow vegetables naturally. You really have to search for this farm. It's somewhere near Secaucus, New Jersey, and it's run by a Jewish farmer who's a retired general. If you find the farm, the next thing you have to do is to pray to God that the farmer has nothing better to do than to deliver that one vegetable to your house personally!

Almost any other food will kill quicker than you can say, "Pass the mustard, Morris."

For example, everybody now knows that red meat is dangerous. Once we believed that if you ate a steak it was good for you. They tried to keep you away from junk foods like popcorn, candy bars and McDonald's French fries.

They said, "Don't eat junk food; eat meat!"

Now they find out that almost nothing is as bad for you as meat. For instance, candy has sugar and sugar is bad for you, but it isn't half as bad as meat. Sugar only gives you diabetes. Not everyone gets it and even if you do get it, you can live quite a while with it.

Red meat gives you cancer, because it has nitrates. And nitrates cause all these things that cause cancer. You can't tell me that cancer is any better for you than diabetes! At least with diabetes you could go for a walk. Where are you going to go with cancer?

So you say to yourself, "Meat is bad for me, so I'll eat something else."

Let's say you decide to eat fish. Well, they found out that all the water in and around America is polluted and almost all the fish contain mercury. And while you eat fish knowing it's great for you and it can help you lose weight, you're dying! Why? Because mercury in fish is one of the greatest menaces to your health. Mercury will kill you.

They tell you that mercury is in every fish in America. So you say to yourself, "I'll stay away from fish. I'll eat chicken!"

Now they found out that the only time it's safe to eat chicken is when you know for a fact the chicken has just died. When the farmers want to make chickens tastier and bigger they give them injections which promote tastier chickens. These injections also cause cancer in the chicken.

So these healthy looking chickens, which are sick with cancer, are going to kill you. But if a chicken looks like it was a miserable looking chicken—you should grab it! Because when a chicken looks unhappy and tastes bad, you will be healthier if you eat it.

I hope you understand this valuable information. The only way for you to live a long life is to eat a sick chicken. There's almost nothing else you can eat that's good for you.

They say carrots are good for your eyes. They *are* good for your eyes—mostly if you look at them from a distance. But if you eat them you're eating a rabbit's favorite food. Did you ever hear of a rabbit who lived long enough to go to an old age home?

I was sitting in my house thinking about this stuff and I realized that even sitting in my house isn't safe. Because if you're over forty and you're sitting still, every minute you sit, you're a minute closer to death. Also, the greatest threat to a person over forty is a heart attack! And you're most likely to get a heart attack because of a lack of exercise.

So even sitting is dangerous. In order to live a long life you have to walk a lot. Walking slow won't help. You have to run to do you any good!

One question is, where will you run? In the street? They found that the streets of our major cities are so clouded with pollution that emphysema has killed more people on the street than muggers!

So you run on the streets of the city to be healthier and to promote a healthier heart. But while you're running your lungs are turning black with pollution poisoning and you're passing away with a healthier heart. Your limbs are getting stronger, your body is getting in shape; every part of your body looks perfect but inside black and green stuff is forming in your lungs.

Now, if you want a good heart without cancer, you do have to run, but not in the street. The smartest thing to do is to run in place in your own house. But don't open the window because you'll be breathing filthy air. Close the window and run in place. Except you'd better do it softly in your apartment or else the guy downstairs will come up and beat on you, which could also be very bad for your health.

As a matter of fact, one day I was running in place in my living room with the windows closed, watching television, and somebody told me that even that isn't safe! They found out that color televisions give off certain rays and if you watch television in your house you could get cancer. Because the color from the set could cause cancer in your body.

You have to stay a certain minimum number of feet away from the set. That's the only way too avoid getting cancer from the rays. The trouble is the safest distance is twenty yards.

You'll have to have two apartments: one for your television set, and another one to watch it from. And then you'd need a pair of binoculars.

I was telling this to my dentist when I realized that he, too, might kill me. Why? Because I found out that the X-rays in this country are causing more deaths than coffee, tea, milk and Coke put together. Do you know that the American people are the most X-rayed people in the world? You're never safe when they're X-raying any part of your body.

They tell you it's safe because every time they take a picture they make a living! But did you notice what the dentist does when he gives you an X-ray?

He says, "Don't worry about it. It's all right."

First he sticks the thing in your mouth and then he runs like hell out of the room! As a matter of fact, he doesn't even come back to talk about it. He doesn't come back to look at it. He calls a laboratory in Philadelphia and asks, "Hello, did the picture come out yet?"

So if a dentist happens to have the television set on and you just happen to have X-rays taken and if perhaps a window is open—all you need is a Coke and someone to call the Campbell Funeral Home for you.

Thinking all these thoughts made me tired. So I put on my pajamas and started to go to bed when I realized that even pajamas can kill you. Pajamas are the most dangerous things to wear to sleep. Pajamas are made with triss, and triss they found out in pajamas is a great cause of cancer!

So remember, when your wife says to you, "I love you darling. Put on your pajamas, have a Coke, and go to bed..." she's really trying to kill you!

Better check where she hides the life insurance policy.

Staying Young

In this country people spend fortunes on salves and lotions trying to look young.

It doesn't help.

There is only one way to look young: hang around with very old people!

Girls and Mountains

Actually, I'm not terribly concerned about whether people like me. The truly successful man is the man who is happy within himself.

Did you know that?

Do you know why I'm blessed with this quality? I'll explain it to you. It's because I'm a happy man. I've found the secret of happiness.

Very few people know how to be happy. That's why so many books are written about the subject. Have you noticed that every time you pick up the newspaper and see ads for books they're about how you can learn to be happy even if it makes you miserable?

I saw a book last week entitled, *How to be Happy Without Money*. The book cost fifteen dollars. It just goes to show that if you have no money, you can't even learn how to be happy without money.

If you could find happiness from books, people wouldn't chase girls. Psychologists figured this out. They had a conference about this in Switzerland. They decided that people climb high mountains to find happiness.

Lots of people chase girls for the same reason that other people climb mountains: to find happiness. Not because they want a girl. They just want to conquer something.

That's the same reason people climb mountains. They need a mountain? Maybe they really do. You couldn't prove it by me.

It's not really the mountain: it's the need for conquest. That's what psychologists figured out in Switzerland when they were surrounded by all that milk chocolate and all those cuckoo clocks.

When people conquer that mountain, they feel happy.

Now, if conquering a girl made you happy, I could see it. That would at least give you something to do.

But what can you do with a conquered mountain? I mean, even if it isn't covered with snow. Once you put the flag in, there's no place to go! Could you invite friends over for the evening to meet your mountain? Could you take a mountain any place? Even if you could, would you want it in the house?

Some of the girls I go out with I wouldn't want in the house either. But given the choice between mountains and girls, I'll take girls anytime.

The Sporting Life

I can never get very excited about sports. I can understand how a person can get excited if he or she is playing. I can understand how a person can get excited if they've made a bet—though gambling always seems to me a foolish business, unless you win. But I can't understand millions of people who don't play or bet and get excited anyway.

Take football. Half of all Americans sit in their homes every weekend all winter watching eleven bruisers meet eleven *shtarkers* dressed up in outfits that would have frightened my grandmother. They call it football, but the object of the game is to bash the other guy so hard that he's eventually carried off the field on a stretcher. This is the way your mother raised her son so he can pay all your money to an orthopedic surgeon?

People who can't name the vice-president of the United States can tell you names, physical dimensions and birthdates of every member of the Cowboys, Raiders, Jets and Eagles, and the names they give to their positions: right end, halfback, fullback, quarterback.

Do you understand this?

Then the season ends. Do you think these people come out onto the streets? Do they enjoy the parks and beaches, the birds and the bees? No, they replace their popcorn supply and watch baseball.

This game, which originated in Africa when tribesmen hit a skull with a stick, is America's pastime. Even Fidel Castro plays it. Sometimes he thinks he's an American.

I have friends who watch eight innings when nothing happens. The score is 0-0. It's the ninth inning. They tell me it's an exciting game.

When you're in New York you have to do like New Yorkers do, so when I'm in Manhattan I become a Yankee or a Met fan. In the winter I'm in Florida. (Should a nice Jewish boy spend his winters in the snow?) I don't understand any of the games but I understand that you are supposed to root for your hometown.

"It isn't important if you win or lose, but it's how you play the game that counts." Can you imagine a team owner telling that to his team? I can't either.

Steve Allen was once asked if he had any proof of the power of prayer. He told about an Army-Navy game where everybody who rooted for Navy prayed that Navy would win. One side won and that proved the power of prayer.

You could have fooled me.

Why I Talk to Myself

People ask why I talk to myself. Do you know anybody more intelligent that I can talk to? Do you know anybody who would be more sympathetic to what I have to say?

I'm very impressed when I listen to myself. I can't get over what a great comedian I am. You know comedians like me don't grow on trees, although I'm told there are a few who swing from them.

You know what I realized only last night? I talk to myself when I'm working in a night club because I discovered half the time the audience isn't listening.

So why should I knock myself out? I cut out the middleman and talk directly to me. And when I talk, I listen. I wait to hear what I have to say. I don't interrupt, because I know I'm dealing with a brilliant fellow.

Why I Talk to Myself

When other people talk, I don't even bother with it. But myself I listen to very carefully. I don't start arguments. No matter what I say, I agree. I'll be honest with you, I know myself so well that if I don't like a subject, I don't even bring it up.

Why should I aggravate myself? I got something stupid to say, I tell it to someone else. Let *them* listen. The more intelligent things, I keep to myself. That's why you're not reading them in this book. But if you buy copies as gifts for all your relatives and friends, maybe I'll relent and tell you the intelligent things in my *next* book.

How I Found Myself and Lost My Psychiatrist

I myself was once self-conscious to such an extent that I couldn't talk to people at all. It's hard to believe. Do you know that if I went to a football game and saw the players go into a huddle, I thought they were talking about me?

I finally went to see a psychiatrist.

I asked him, "What will this cost me?"

He told me, "Seventy-five dollars a visit."

I said, "For seventy-five dollars I don't visit, I move in!"

Then he took out an ink blot and he said to me, "What do you see in this ink blot?"

I said, "I see that you need a new fountain pen."

For seventy-five dollars, I figured I'll drive *him* crazy.

He told me to lie on the couch.

Then he said, "Tell me what's bothering you?"

I said, "Your seventy-five-dollar fee for the visit."

So he said, "I understand your problem. Your insecurity about money is because you hate your sister."

I told him, "But I haven't got a sister."

He said, "I see you're going to be a difficult patient. I'm not going to be able to help you if you don't cooperate."

Then he said, "I'll ask you another question. Why do you despise your father?"

I said, "It so happens that I have a lot of respect for my father."

He said, "All right. All right! Tell me then why you hate your mother?"

I said, "I love my mother."

"You see! You aren't cooperating!" he said. "You have to stop resisting me. Otherwise we'll never get anywhere. I want you to tell me when you first started to hate your brother."

I said, "I don't hate my brother. I love my brother."

He said, "Do you have a cousin you hate?"

I told him: "No. I love everybody."

"Ah ha!" he said. "You see! That's your trouble. You're maladjusted. You see, you *have* to hate somebody to be normal."

I said, "To tell you the truth, right now, I'm not so crazy about you."

He said, "From all your cousins, you can't pick out one cousin you hate? Is that asking too much?"

I didn't answer him.

He said, "Usually I ask for three or four cousins. I'm only asking you for one lousy cousin. You can't help me out?"

I said, "I can't help you. I happen to have wonderful cousins." "Maybe *you* have a cousin you hate?"

He said, "As a matter of fact, I do."

I said, "Then we've discovered *your* problem."

I said, "So you have. What do you suggest we do about it?"

I said, "Lie down on the couch. Maybe *I* could help *you*."

He said, "What is it?"

I said, "It's seventy-five dollars a visit."

He exploded: "No therapist is worth seventy-five dollars a visit!"

Then he wanted to know if I was normal with regard to women. So he said to me: "A very simple question. When you meet a girl, what's the first thing that you look for?"

"A hotel room," I said.

He said, "That's not normal. I'm talking about love. I want to know if you had a true love relationship with any one girl."

I said, "Positively."

He asked, "What was her name?"

"I don't remember."

"Do you remember her address?"

I said, "I don't remember that either."

He said, "You aren't helping me. I've decided that you feel deprived because people don't love you. You're hungry for love."

Maybe he was telling the truth. My mother had a

terrible problem. It just so happened that she didn't know how to express love. Many women in this country suffer from that problem.

Modern technology has created a situation where women know how to play video games but they don't know how to express love. Have you noticed this? You haven't? This is one of the greatest problems and I want you to spend time thinking about it.

A professor from Columbia University is the one who discovered this. He travelled around the country to see what percentage of the women in America really know how to express love, and he found out personally.

In his last message, this professor reported that three out of four women have no idea how to express love. The professor never returned but they're not looking for him. They're looking for that fourth woman.

If I could find that fourth woman, would I need a professor?

You understand what I'm talking about?

Now, what do you think happened because my mother hated me and my father hated me and people in general couldn't stand me? I began to suspect I wasn't popular.

So the psychiatrist told me that I had to find *something* to fall in love with. He told me to search my unconscious.

That's when I discovered that I had a thing for my galoshes. Don't laugh. I know it sounds ridiculous saying I had a relationship with my galoshes. How could I love galoshes? Okay. I *like* my galoshes.

I'll tell you one thing: I got beautiful galoshes. I wouldn't be foolish enough to tell you I love them, but I'll admit I hug them once in a while.

Don't get me wrong: I would *never* kiss them. That would be abnormal. How could a grown man love galoshes? I love my umbrella! My galoshes are nothing compared to my umbrella.

If you saw my umbrella, you wouldn't bother with galoshes either. You want me to be honest with you? I never even wanted to take out my galoshes. I was ashamed. How does it look? I *always* take out my umbrella and I don't bother with my galoshes. So once in a while I take out my galoshes. But I never *really* was in love with them.

Let's face it. Galoshes look like nothing. An umbrella, that looks like something.

"How do you do? I want you to meet my umbrella. Sweet, isn't she?"

An umbrella comes in different colors. You could pass off an umbrella for a celebrity. Twiggy, maybe.

Above everything else, remember this: find out who you are. Most people never find out who they are.

There was a time when even I didn't know who I was. It's hard to believe. Lucky for me, my psychiatrist told me who I am. If it wasn't for him, I wouldn't know who I am to this day.

That's the truth. As soon as I walked into his office, he said to me, "We're going to have to find out who the real you is. Otherwise you'll never be happy."

I couldn't figure it out at the time.

I said to myself, "I need him to find out who I am? If I don't know who I am, how is he going to know? He never met me before."

"You don't know me,," I told him.

He said, "We both don't know you, that's why we have to search for the real you!"

I said to myself, "If I don't know who I am, how would I know what I look like? And even if I find me, how would I know it's me? Besides, if I want to look for me, why do I need him? I could look myself or I could call my friends. They could help me look!"

Where would I tell them to start?

"Besides," I told myself, "what if I find the real me, and I find that he's even worse than I am. Why do I need him? I don't make enough for myself—I need a partner? Ten years ago I'd been glad to look for anybody, but now I'm doing good. Why should I look for him? Let him look for me!"

The psychiatrist said, "The search for the real you will continue at our next session. That will be seventy-five dollars."

I said to myself, "This is not the real me. Why should *I* give him seventy-five dollars? What if I find the real me and he doesn't think it's worth seventy-five dollars? Then I wasted my money for the real him. . . ."

I told myself, "For all I know, the real me might be going to a different psychiatrist altogether. In fact, he might even be this psychiatrist himself!"

I said to him, "What if *you're* the real me! Then you owe me seventy-five dollars."

"Go," he said. "If you promise never to come back, we'll call it even."

He slammed the door in my face.

If you run into the real me, tell him what happened. Tell him I can't afford to search for him anymore so he has to show up by himself.

Tell him I'll wait for him right here.

Status Seeking

Everything today is a matter of status. People don't just want to keep up with the Cohens and Kellys, they want to look down on them.

In the old days, a family who couldn't afford a television set would at least buy an antenna. That way everybody would *think* they had a TV. Sometimes a family would sit for hours at a time with their backs to the front window so that the neighbors would think they had a set.

Then came air-conditioning in cars. I know a fellow who couldn't afford air-conditioning but he didn't want his friends to know that. So he would drive through the neighborhood on the hottest days with his car windows closed tight. He sweated off ten pounds every summer.

I've been talking about the men but women aren't much

different in this department. Don't you know ladies who carry Gucci bags but stuff 'em with merchandise from Alexanders?

We're all searching for an image. Philip Wylie once reported on a man who walked into a hat shop and happened to try on a cowboy hat. The next thing you know, he bought a large ranch and dressed in cowboy clothes all the time. And this was in the Bronx!

The newest thing is to buy designer labels. You buy a Calvin Klein label and sew it onto Brand "X" jeans. It's getting so that you have to do that because designer clothes are so expensive. Did you know that even Gloria Vanderbilt can't afford Gloria Vanderbilt jeans? She shops at J.C. Penney.

Now we're into reverse snobbism. In the old days the idea was to dress to look as sharp as you could. So we got all our styles from Harlem.

That's right. We'd give our old clothes to our maids—especially the ones who did windows. They'd take 'em home to their boyfriends. The boyfriends would put together a coat from here and a tie from there and that's how style was born.

Soon the blacks were copying the whites and the whites were copying the blacks and nobody knew how to dress. It was a standoff.

The rock bands brought the solution. The rock musicians came onto the stage so zonked out with drugs that they forgot to dress. Friends would put them into *something*, just so they wouldn't be arrested for exhibitionism.

This became style. The worse you looked, the better you looked. Everybody tried to look dirty and sloppy.

Bums on the Bowery became millionaires posing for *Vogue* and *Gentleman's Quarterly*. Whole industries sprang up whose only function was to rip shirts, stomp on coats, and trample on jeans.

The only one who didn't get with the style was the president. He was so busy in the White House watching his old movies that he didn't notice everybody looked destitute.

So he didn't do anything and soon everybody *was* destitute.

Now the time came when he was told he had to face a crisis. There was a problem in Lebanon. So he flew Danny Thomas to Washington for advice on the Lebanese crisis.

It's true! The future of United States relations with Lebanon hung on the advice of Danny Thomas.

Now Danny Thomas had status.

He could look down at Sammy Davis. To begin with, Thomas is taller. But the kicker is, did President Reagan ever invite Sammy Davis to the White House to advise him on the Israeli crisis?

Never!

I think the Anti-Defamation League should get in on this one.

Come Swing With Me and I'm Not Talking About the Playground in Central Park

The singles scene has become Desperation Alley. People who don't drink or can't dance or are too shy to talk to strangers in bars and discos are turning instead to the singles magazines.

These magazines contain page after page packed with personal ads. These ads are not only personal, they are anonymous too. In fact, they're so private most of them only give you a box number—because God forbid you should become so turned on by the ad you decide to show up on the writer's doorstep.

I hesitate to quote them in a national best-selling family book like this. What if my mother happens to read this chapter? What if she answers the ads?

The "girl wanted" ads seem all to have been placed by lazy Lotharios who got the hots and want to locate innocent herpes-free nymphomaniacs. Here's a sample:

> BROADMINDED, UNINHIBITED, LOVE-STARVED MAN IS HOT-TO-TROT WITH SEXY GIRL HAVING BIG TITS AND A LARGE ASS. INTERESTS INCLUDE INDOOR NUDISM. NO TIME FOR LONG COURTSHIP BECAUSE I'M AT THE END OF MY ROPE.

This bum, when he meets the girl for the first time, wants to start unbuttoning his pants with one hand while he's shaking hands with the other. This guy is definitely not a very good prospect for marriage.

The women have their ads too.

> STAGGERINGLY BEAUTIFUL, DEVASTATINGLY SEXY LADY, BUILT LIKE YOU-KNOW-WHAT SEEKS HANDSOME, RICH MAN TO TAKE HER TO LAS VEGAS. NO CHEAPSKATES! I CAN GET ALL THE CHEAPIES I WANT DOWN AT P.J. COHEN'S BAR ON THE CORNER. IF YOU CAN'T TAKE ME OUT IN THE MANNER I EXPECT, DON'T EXPECT TO TAKE ME.

Then, of course, there are couples looking for couples. The way these ads read, some fellow and his wife are ready for full-blown orgies in the middle of Collins Avenue at lunchtime.

SWINGING COUPLE EAGER TO MEET ONE OR MORE OTHER COUPLES FOR COMPLEX COUPLINGS. THE MORE THE MERRIER! WE FIRMLY BELIEVE THAT WHAT TWO CAN DO WELL, TWELVE CAN DO BETTER!

Not all the swinging couples want crowds. Some just need one more girl to join them in bed. Maybe the wife did too much housework. Or maybe the kids tired her out. Like this one:

"DARLING, WE NEED YOU!" FUN-LOVING COUPLE SEEKS FUN-LOVING FEMALE FOR FUN-FILLED FROLICS FOR THREE. WE'D LOVE TO HAVE YOU ABOARD.

I feel sorry for the man in this trio. He has to perform like an organ-grinder's trained monkey. Me? They couldn't pay me enough to entertain two women at the same time in a locked bedroom unless, of course, one of the women happened to be Sophia Loren. In which case, you and I should talk about it.

Not all the ads are so forthright. For example, the other night, while I was watching a replay of an old Ed Sullivan show on television, I came upon this one:

NICE SHY BOY WITH JEWISH MOTHER IN PERPETUAL ATTENDANCE WOULD LIKE A NICE

SHY JEWISH GIRL TO JOIN HIM AT A FREE PARK CONCERT. OKAY TO BRING ALONG YOUR NICE JEWISH SISTER. WILL TREAT ALL TO LEMONADES AT THE AUTOMAT AFTER THE CONCERT.

What's the matter with this guy? Doesn't he want steamy action? Isn't X-rated a good enough rating for him? This one I personally wouldn't suggest you respond to.

Write to me instead.

Did My Service Answer?

In this age of technological wizardry, everything is electronics! And now every home has a machine to answer the telephone.

Even people who four years ago complained to you about speaking to a telephone answering machine and would never leave a message have their own phone answering machines today.

Do you know why? I'll tell you why? They're sick of answering services!

You don't mind talking into a machine now. As boring as it is, at least you know the other person could get your message if he wanted to.

Did My Service Answer?

Did you ever try to leave a message with an answering service? Ha!

Everyone who works for an answering service is trained to get even with you for disturbing them. They don't feel it's a job they're being paid to do. They all act like they have a job at night and they do this daytimes as a prison sentence. They were sentenced by some judge in Chicago to answer the phone and take messages.

When I call someone and they have an answering service, I pray the service people don't pick up! Usually I don't have a problem because nine out of ten times they won't. And if they do pick it up, it's on the thirty-fourth ring. You're relieved and you say to yourself, "Thank God, I got them!"

But you don't get a chance to say anything because as soon as they pick up the phone they all say the same thing: "Could you please hold on."

Except that's not what they say. They actually issue the command: "Hold on!" They're trained not to use the word "please."

You're left wondering, "Should I risk another half hour waiting for them to pick up again? Maybe I should phone someone else?"

Fifteen minutes later they pick up again, and you have a wonderful sense of triumph. You've been rewarded for your infinite patience.

Unfortunately, by now they're angry at you for bothering them twice! They act like they owe you money and you came to collect!

I don't even know the lady answering the phone! She doesn't owe me anything. She doesn't even know me. Why is she cursing me?

So she begins: "Mr. Irving's residence."

You hear the resentment in her voice right away. She hates Irving more than she hates you. And if you ask, "Is he in?" She answers, "Listen, mister, if he were in, would I be answering his telephone?"

She doesn't exactly say those words but you can hear the message in her attitude. If you dare say, "I'd like to leave a message." she responds abruptly: "Hold on!"

I would like to know why she has time to chat with me until I want to leave a message. Then, suddenly, she's busy again. It's a message service. Don't the bosses furnish her with a pencil? Is she doing another job on the side? Maybe she's selling shirts while she's taking messages?

To leave a message would take a second and a half; for her to come back takes a week. I always want to tell her "You hold on, I'll be right back." But my advice is don't ever do that. You'll never hear from her again.

So automatic phone machines have become a big hit because people are fed up with answering services. And the reason people like to buy an answering machine is because it's a good way to let people know you could afford one.

I know somebody who can't afford one and he's so ashamed that when you call his apartment, he pretends to be a machine.

With a good machine you can impress people before they even talk to you. Normally you have to talk to someone for at least twenty minutes to make an impression. The machine gives you thirty seconds to make any impression you want! And the caller is a captive audience because he's waiting to leave you a message.

One guy was trying to show how important he was when I called him last week. The machine answered like this: "Hello. I had to sell my Rolls-Royce so I left my two-million-dollar house for a few minutes but it's all right because I have this seven-thousand-dollar answering machine called the Commodore Executive System which will forward my calls anywhere in the world except Bali and my bank vault. At the moment, I'm in my bank vault clipping coupons.

"If this is an emergency, contact my mother! She still lives on the Concourse in the Bronx. I know the neighborhood's changed but so did my mother. And don't call Paul Newman looking for me because he's not home. He's out looking for me. And if I don't have time for Paul Newman, why do you think I have time for you? Fuck you and Paul Newman!"

You can always tell when a person is desperate and lonely by the message he puts on his machine. He or she says something like: "Thank you for calling. I appreciate it. I'm sorry I'm not here but thanks, anyway. Just the fact that you thought of me is nice to know and I thank you for calling now, and thank you for the next time you think enough of me to do it.

"I'm sorry you didn't call yesterday because I wasn't doing anything yesterday, but if you don't happen to get me now, call me tomorrow because, through a lucky coincidence, chances are I'll be doing nothing again!"

Okay, now it's your turn. Start talking when you hear the beep.